Happy 60th Birthday Rich -

We hope you enjoy this book as we know you enjoy the tour every year!

Paul and Judy Neussl

INSIDE THE
TOUR DE FRANCE

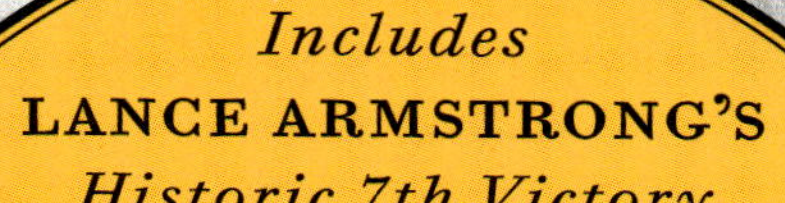

Includes
LANCE ARMSTRONG'S
Historic 7th Victory
and His Final Professional Race

INSIDE THE TOUR DE FRANCE

The Pictures, the Legends, and the Untold Stories of the World's Most Beloved Bicycle Race

ERIC DELANZY

NOTICE

Mention of specific companies, organizations, or authorities in this book does not imply endorsement by the publisher, nor does mention of specific companies, organizations, or authorities imply that they endorse this book.

Printed in the United States of America

Rodale Inc. makes every effort to
use acid-free ♾, recycled paper ♻.

Book design by Susan P. Eugster

Library of Congress Cataloging-in-Publication Data

Delanzy, Eric.
Inside the Tour de France : the pictures, the legends, and the untold stories of the world's most beloved bicycle race / Eric Delanzy.
p. cm.
Includes index.
ISBN-13 978-1-59486-230-4 hardcover
ISBN-10 1-59486-230-3 hardcover
1. Tour de France (Bicycle race)–History. 2. Tour de France (Bicycle race)–Pictorial works. 3. Cyclists–Biography. I. Title.
GV1049.2.T68D44 2006
796.6'20944–dc22 2006002345

Distributed to the book trade by Holtzbrinck Publishers

2 4 6 8 10 9 7 5 3 1 hardcover

We inspire and enable people to improve their lives and the world around them

For more of our products visit **rodalestore.com** or call 800-848-4735

BP
BP

CONTENTS

FOREWORD

Since its inception in 1903, the Tour de France has captured the imagination of the world. Le Grand Bouclé, or the Big Loop, has challenged the world's greatest athletes for more than 100 years to produce superhuman feats of endurance and speed. Men have risked limb and life to have their names written in stars across the heavens, along the serpentine and ever lethal roads of the Tour.

Every foible, folly, and corruption that the human heart is capable of is pitifully visible for the world to see during the Tour. Yet, every courageous, chivalrous, and astute, fraternal and generous impulse of the human condition is also offered up to an adoring public with more clarity than in any other sport.

A privately held yet primordial human emotion is the fear of being left behind by the pack. One of the most pitiful and mournful sights in all sports is the lone Tour man regurgitated out of the back of the peleton to ride without its protection. This happenstance never ceases to reach into the depths of our own fears, resonating to an ancient time when being left behind meant death.

From those depths also comes the glory of the Tour, in which a man is capable of launching himself away from the charging mass. The exhilarating attacks, whereby a man of supreme conviction and strength separates himself from the sheltering pack, have become the fuel of legends.

These two extremes—the fear and the exhilaration—wage war for our attention and sympathy every day of each Tour de France. The men who are capable of destroying the resolve of their competitors—by cunning and sheer strength, by patience and absolute audacity, by subterfuge and complete confidence—have become modern mankind's greatest sporting heroes. Their exploits sustained a populace devastated after two World Wars and a worldwide depression and inspire us today with a dynamic, ever colorful, and multinational spectacle of grandeur, cooperation, and grace.

The men left behind by fatigue, injury, and even death provide us with a constant reminder of the frailty of our perch on this life, how tenuous our grasp is on this world.

The glorious champions and those horribly vanquished riders are so closely entwined at the Tour that our hearts can barely discern which is which. Even the villanous winners and beautiful losers entrall us. We are a communion of saints picnicking on a sunny hillside as a procession of martyrs march by.

For the riders, the Tour's grind is barely survivable. But watching this disintegration of the best and brightest allows us to escape our own day-to-day drudgery. Why the Tour de France resounds powerfully for its fans is that these men refuse to surrender in spite of each exhausting pedal stroke. By witnessing their resolve, we can endure; by seeing them strive, we can imagine our own rewards just over each horizon.

—Bob Roll

PREFACE

The history of the Tour de France is in many ways synonymous with the history of France. In our hearts and minds, the wartime battles of François I, Louis the XIV, and Napoléon I can be compared with the on-the-bike feats of Maurice Garin and Nicolas Frantz, the dogged race tactics of Gino Bartali and Louison Bobet, and the fearsome assaults of Eddy Merckx and Bernard Hinault. The Galibier is our Waterloo; the Tourmalet is Omaha Beach!

It's an extreme analogy, but it's a valid one. As every schoolboy is taught, battle is the landmark of our history, shaping the centuries with tremendous victories and tragic losses. For cycling fans, the Tour de France is immortalized by the exploits of its champions.

But an event as rich, elaborate, and monumental as the Tour de France cannot be distilled to just the tales of its greatest winners and its biggest battles. For a true history, you need the anecdotes: the overlooked tales of valor, the little-known riders, the behind-the-scenes moments—stolen by a microphone or passed on from ear to ear—that create the legend of the race.

Today, television cameras see (almost) everything that happens during the Tour de France. But the race still has a colorful backstage: the riders with their joys and their pains; the emotion and the iron will of the race. That is why the Tour de France has lived beyond 100 and why it will continue to thrive.

This book by Timée Editions is a remarkable and original idea: to collect and classify the top moments of the Tour de France, a combination of the great and small "magic moments" of the race.

In reading these pages, it will be difficult not to give in to fascination. You will sometimes smile and sometimes grimace as you are captured by the diversity of this trove of Tour de France treasures. Read the tales—the stories from antiquity and those from the modern day—in order or out of order. When you've finished, you'll see that in addition to the values of our sport—courage, dedication, altruism—there's a common thread that ties together all the tales in this anthology: love.

—**JEAN-MARIE LEBLANC,**
Race Director of the Tour de France

CHAPTER 1

A Historic—and Heroic—Debut

On July 1, 1903, the world of cycling entered a new era. Based on a brainstorm by journalist Géo Lefèvre, Henri Desgrange—director of the French sports newspaper L'Auto*—rolled out the first Tour de France. Sixty riders lined up for the race's maiden voyage.*

Maurice Garin, winner of the inaugural Tour de France, savors his race spoils alongside his son.

A Political Tour

Paris, Lyon, Marseille, Toulouse, Bordeaux, Nantes, Paris. The first Tour de France, in 1903, was six stages long. But the race may never have been without the political turmoil surrounding the Dreyfus Affair.

At the dawn of the 20th century, French opinion was divided between those who condemned and those who supported Alfred Dreyfus, a French military captain charged with selling secrets to Germany. Every sector of the population was sucked into the divide. The debate raged from political pulpits to sports stadiums. But no one expected that this national turmoil would give birth to the world's greatest sporting event.

At the dawn of its day, the bicycle was known as the velocipede, an instrument of luxury coveted by the social elite and a technical marvel that helped make the fortunes of captains of industry such as Dunlop, Clément, and Michelin.

The first cycling races were organized by the press, each newspaper seeking to cajole a maximum number of readers for the coverage of its sponsored event. The powerful daily *Vélo,* created in 1892 by Pierre Giffard, could boast the major players of industry among its shareholders: Michelin, for one, as well as Albert De Dion and his cohorts, makers of automobiles.

But there was a rub: Giffard was pro Alfred Dreyfus, firmly defending the military captain charged with treason (unjustly, it turned out, as he was acquitted in 1899). France's deep division on the Dreyfus Affair extended to the columns of Giffard's newspaper, causing a rift with the vehemently anti-Dreyfus De Dion.

On October 16, 1900, De Dion launched *L'Auto* as a direct competitor of *Vélo.* The result was all-out war for bike-race dominance. *Vélo* organized a Bordeaux-to-Paris race, and *L'Auto* quickly followed suit, promising better racers and faster times.

And in the end, it was *L'Auto* that got the last word. In 1902, Henri Desgrange and Victor Goddet, the paper's editorial masterminds, hatched the idea of a Tour de France. A year later, the first edition of the now-famous race rolled out, counting six stages that averaged 250 miles each. The race was a triumph, and *L'Auto* (which evolved into the modern French sports daily *L'Equipe*) won the publishing war, forcing *Vélo* into bankruptcy.

L'Auto

AUTOMOBILE — CYCLISME

LE TOUR DE FRANCE — LE DÉPART

Organisé par L'AUTO du 1er au 19 Juillet 1903

LA SEMENCE

L'ITINÉRAIRE DU TOUR DE FRANCE

QUI?

The front page of *L'Auto* newspaper was dedicated to the biggest event on the 1903 sports calendar: the start of the first Tour de France.

I

On a Bed of Nails

The Tour de France is exhausting, both physically and mentally. Surviving the difficulties of the course and its contestants is one thing. Surviving the malicious humor of the fans is another.

Lucien Petit-Breton *(left)* returns to the race after a brief desertion.

In 1905, race organizers hoped to be past the shenanigans of sabotage that had marred the previous Tour de France. Disaster, however, struck from the very first stage of the race on July 9. Just outside of Meaux, the riders pedaled onto a literal bed of nails, some 275 pounds of the little spikes blanketing the road.

The incident was an annoyance for the professional riders in the race. But for the amateurs—who had little or no access to spare bike parts—it was a catastrophe. The vast majority of the amateur field rolled to the stage's end in Nancy outside the time delay allowed by Tour de France organizers.

The race was pitched into chaos, and its furious director, Henri Desgrange, was on the verge of bringing it to a premature end. Desgrange's entourage and a number of racers eventually convinced him otherwise. The day after the nail-bitten stage—a rest day on the race—Desgrange announced that all of the riders eliminated due to the time delay would be reintegrated into the peloton.

In the counting of the race's ranks, however, one rider was still missing: Lucien Petit-Breton, one of the overall favorites.

Discouraged and convinced that he had been eliminated from the race, Petit-Breton had taken a train to Paris. When he learned of the about-face decision by Desgrange to reinstate all the competitors, Petit-Breton made a mad dash back to Nancy. He was slapped with a 70-point penalty but was allowed to take the start of the second stage.

In the end, Petit-Breton finished fifth in his first-ever Tour de France—without ever crossing the finish line of the race's first stage!

An engineer from Toulouse made a sales pitch before the start of the third edition of the Tour de France: He proposed equipping the racers with a "revolutionary" antipuncture, nail-removing tool of his own invention. None of the contestants took him up on his offer. They probably should have.

Discouraged by obstacles out of their control, the riders of the 1905 Tour nonetheless didn't give in.

I

Faber: First Foreigner

In 1909, François Faber became one of the French public's first Tour de France heroes. But was he really one of their own?

His bicycle's chain broken, François Faber hoofed it to the finish in Lyon.

In the 1909 Tour de France, one rider rose above the rest: François Faber, a giant of a man who won five consecutive stages at the start of the race. It was an unprecedented feat and one that inspired the adulation of the public. There was just one small detail his fans didn't know.

In 1909, François Faber had a stranglehold on the Tour de France. He was nearly invincible in the mountains, which, considering his size (6 foot 1 inch and 200 pounds), was a shock to the race's flyweights. Faber, however, was untouchable—even in the most adverse conditions, as proved by his stage win in Lyon on July 11.

Braving hail and extreme cold, Faber broke away. Seemingly free of the peloton, Faber came to a screeching halt less than a mile from the finish line: The chain of his bicycle, strained by caked-on mud, had snapped in two. Faber didn't lose a second. Instead of waiting for assistance, he ran, holding his bike with one hand. He won the stage on foot.

An all-around racer, Faber also earned kudos for his sportsmanship. He shared his midstage feedbag with other competitors, and when no food was to be found, he twice made forays to find sustenance for exhausted riders.

Faber was just as generous with stage victories. After piling up his own triumphs, he worked to help his teammates and his half brother, Ernest Paul, achieve wins of their own.

As far as the French public was concerned, Faber was the perfect racer. They were thrilled to count him as one of their own. But therein lay Faber's rub: Despite living in France, Faber, it turned out, was born in Luxembourg.

Having forgotten to select French citizenship when he became an adult, Faber unwittingly became the first foreigner to win a Tour de France. That accolade, however, didn't stop him from dying for France in World War I.

A hero on the bike, Faber was also a hero in war. He volunteered to serve and fell to enemy bullets while attempting to carry an injured soldier to safety.

Faber, Louis Trousselier, and Cyrille Van Houwaert enjoying a rest day in Biarritz

Killer Pyrenees

At its dawn, the Tour ignored the Pyrenees, preferring the hills of Alsace and certain Alpine summits. It's easy to see why.

Future Tour winner Octave Lapize confronts the Aubisque climb.

Today, a Tour de France without the Alps or the Pyrenees is inconceivable. The legend of the Tour was made in those mountains, and they are now an integral part of the race. That, however, wasn't the case in the early years of the Tour de France. When race organizers looked to the high hills in 1910, rider reaction boiled down to one word: "Assassins!"

Scene: The office of Henri Desgrange. The Tour de France boss is mulling over the 1910 race route with one of his collaborators, Alphonse Steines, who wants to broaden the race's horizons.

Steines: "I think we should explore the borders of the country."

Desgrange: "Easier said than done, Steines. There's no problem with going north, but to the south are the Pyrenees."

Steines: "Exactly! The race should tackle the Pyrenees."

Desgrange: "You're crazy, my poor Steines. Take some time off to get your head straight."

At the time, Steines's Pyrenean proposition did seem ludicrous. In 1910, the Pyrenees were a vast mountain wall with few inhabitants and even fewer roads.

Steines, however, didn't give up. He took the time off recommended by his boss for a winter reconnaissance trip to the Pyrenees. Hiking around the village of Sainte-Marie de Campan, Steines was overwhelmed by the icy beauty of the mountains. Steines was so enamored with the scenery that he didn't notice the setting sun.

The next morning, a police patrol found Steines half-dead from hypothermia. Between his chattering teeth, Steines stuttered, "Everything's fine . . . The race will climb the Tourmalet."

Back to health, Steines still had the task of convincing Desgrange, who replied, "You're even crazier than I thought! Force the cyclists to climb what amounts to goat trails . . . Who do you think is going to take the wrath of the riders? Me, that's who!"

Yet Desgrange finally agreed to include the Pyrenees in the 1910 Tour. On the day before the gargantuan mountain stage between Luchon and Bayonne—203 miles over four 5,000-foot summits—however, Desgrange suddenly proclaimed himself sick, citing work-induced exhaustion.

It was Steines who took the wrath of the racers, smacked by a scream of "Assassins!" by the future winner, Octave Lapize, at the summit of the Aubisque.

Alphonse Steines *(right)*, the guilty party who introduced the Pyrenees to the Tour de France

Crime and No Punishment

Some riders will do anything to win the Tour de France. And if the fans find a cheat, they won't hesitate to point an accusatory finger.

Poison victim Paul Duboc during the stage between Luchon and Bayonne

In the first Tours de France, the battle for the win often resorted to anything-goes tactics. The most blatant example was during the 1911 edition of the race: a dismaying tale involving the top two riders in the overall standings, vicious rumors, and a mysterious potion.

At the start of the Pyrenean stage between Luchon and Bayonne on July 21, the race leader, Paul Duboc, confirmed his flying form. An outsider for the overall win, Duboc made mincemeat of the Peyresourde summit and relegated his runner-up, Gustave Garrigou, to a deficit of more than 8 minutes at the top of the Tourmalet.

Riding ever further into the lead, Duboc hit the opening grades of the Aubisque climb when, suddenly, the Frenchman turned ghost white and began an erratic zigzag trajectory before crashing to the roadside. Convulsed by horrid attacks of vomiting, a haggard Duboc wallowed in sickness for over an hour before finding his wits and continuing with the race.

What happened to Duboc? The mystery remains to this day, but several rumors run rampant. Some say his trainer concocted a "pick-me-up" with a tad too much kick—in other words, a miscalculated dose of a doping product. The most popular hypothesis, however, was that Duboc was handed a poisoned water bottle at the feed zone in Argelès.

Suspicious eyes turned toward Garrigou, the obvious benefactor if Duboc would have been KO'd. And even if there was no proof of his wrongdoing, Garrigou became public enemy number one for a large portion of the race's fans.

Garrigou already had detractors well before he was accused of poisoning Duboc. From a bourgeois background, Garrigou was in stark contrast to the proletariat countrymen who made up the rest of the pack. He was nicknamed "the Dandy" and enjoyed the pretentious luxury of having trunks of clean clothes shipped to several stage stops on the race route.

The final stage of the Tour de France traversed the city of Rouen—Duboc's hometown. The suspicious Rouen public didn't exactly roll out the red carpet for Garrigou: The race leader decided, for security's sake, to camouflage himself by wearing a different race jersey and removing his race numbers. His strategy worked. Protected by three vehicles, Garrigou got through Rouen undetected. He won the race, but the question of his integrity remained.

Gustave Garrigou making sure his drink is poison free.

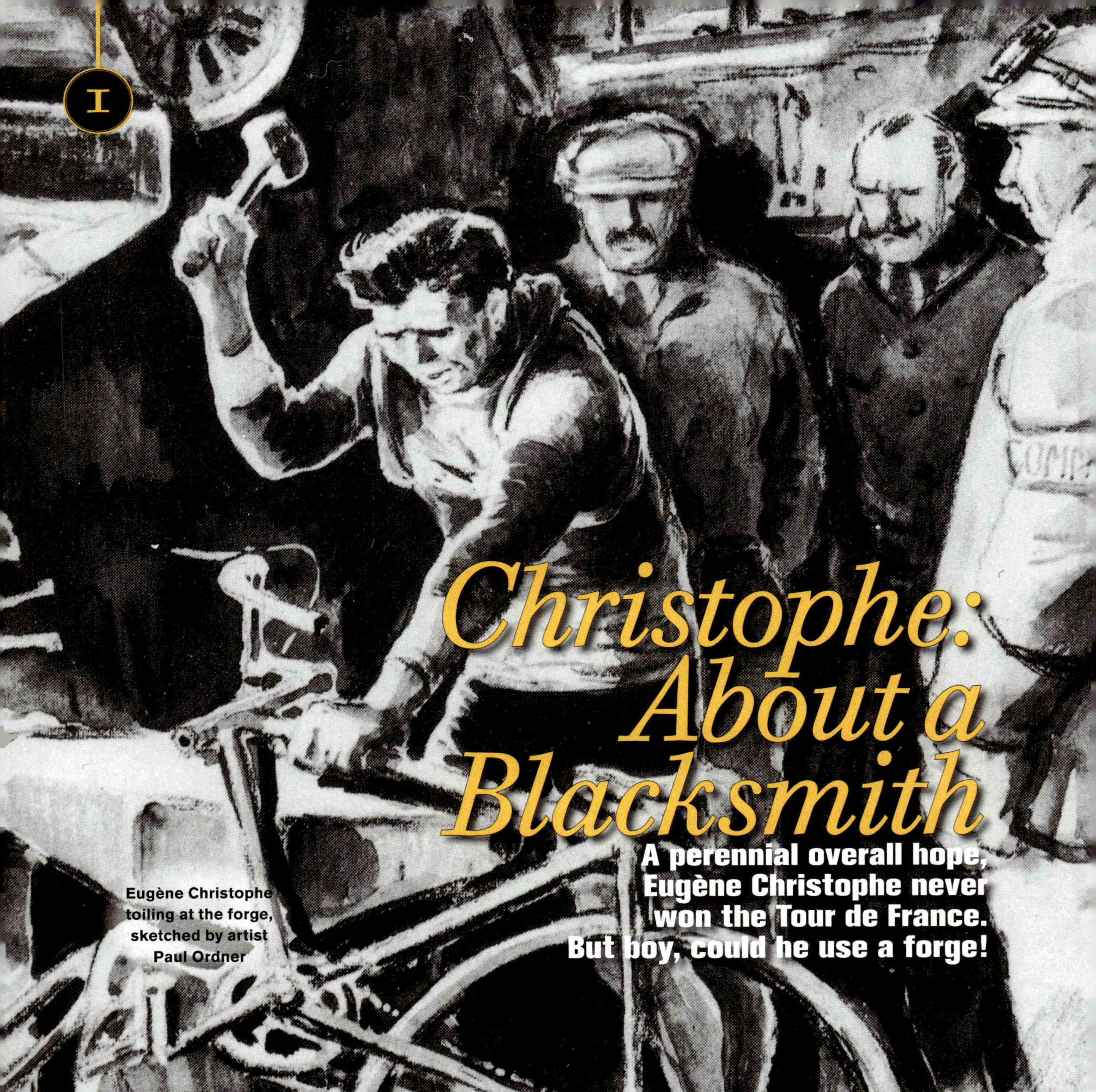

I

Christophe: About a Blacksmith

A perennial overall hope, Eugène Christophe never won the Tour de France. But boy, could he use a forge!

Eugène Christophe toiling at the forge, sketched by artist Paul Ordner

A race revelation and second in the classification by points in 1912, Eugène Christophe badly wanted to win the Tour de France in 1913. His chances were boosted when race director Henri Desgrange reinstated the rule that the overall standings would be decided by fastest overall elapsed time—an amendment that would have handed victory to Christophe the year before. However, to Christophe's chagrin, there was another very specific rule in the Tour de France race book that remained the same.

On July 9, 1913, all of the favorites were in the mix, racing for victory on the Tour's major Pyrenean stage: a vicious mountain haul between Bayonne and Luchon. Cresting the summit of the Tourmalet, Eugène Christophe was in an elite group, shouldered by Philippe Thys, Lucien Petit-Breton, Gustave Garrigou, and Firmin Lambot—all of them former or future Tour de France winners.

While attacking the descent, Christophe was surprised by a close-passing car and crashed. The rider was unhurt, but his bike was destroyed, its fork completely sawed off. Reduced to walking, Christophe hoofed 9 miles to the nearest village, Sainte-Marie de Campan, and headed straight to the town's blacksmith.

The race rules of the day prohibited outside technical assistance. Christophe would have to melt his own iron and reshape and reattach his fork all by his lonesome—and under the watchful eye of race officials.

When one of the judges tried to excuse himself to buy a sandwich, Christophe blew a gasket: "If you're hungry, eat some coal! As long as I'm your prisoner, the only thing you'll do is watch."

In the end, the pit stop cost Christophe 4 hours on the race clock—plus a 3-minute penalty later slapped on because a town schoolboy had helped Christophe keep the forge's fire stoked.

Despite the debacle, Christophe's persistence paid off: The Frenchman rode to an honorable seventh in the final overall standings.

Christophe, the victim of a mechanical mishap

I

The First Yellow Jersey

For years there was no way to distinguish the leader of the Tour de France pack. Then came the yellow jersey . . .

Eugène Christophe leading a breakaway in the Pyrenees. Was he really the first man to wear yellow in Tour history?

A Tour de France without the yellow jersey. Unthinkable? Think again. Contrary to popular belief, the yellow jersey did not debut with the inaugural edition of the race in 1903. When was the iconoclastic jersey first introduced? Good question . . .

In 1919, popular opinion demanded a solution for spotting the Tour de France's race leader, too easily lost in the mass of the pack. Journalists suggested that race director Henri Desgrange invent a distinctive leader's jersey. Desgrange agreed. After all, the race was proving to be a roaring success: All facets of the media were interested in the Tour de France, more and more spectators were flocking to the roadside, and the number of participants was also on the rise.

As Desgrange's newspaper, *L'Auto*, was printed on yellow paper, yellow was the chosen color for the leader's jersey.

On July 19, 1919, in Grenoble, Frenchman Eugène Christophe pulled on the first yellow jersey in the race's history. Most historians agree with this rendition of the yellow-jersey tale, but not all.

Another rider, Philippe Thys, remembered wearing the yellow jersey in 1913. Thys, the first triple winner of the Tour de France (1913, 1914, 1920), claimed that he had, at first, refused to wear a gold-colored leader's jersey, worried that he'd become a sitting-duck target for the rest of the race. Desgrange and Thys's team director insisted, and the Belgian eventually capitulated, donning a poorly sized yellow jersey.

"I had to cut a slit down the collar to fit my head through, which is how I ended up riding several stages with the plunging neckline of a woman's dress," Thys said.

Today, due to a dearth of firsthand witnesses, Thys's yellow-jersey claims can't be ratified. But according to numerous Tour historians, Thys was a reliable source. And after all, there is a thread of logic through his tale. It would seem plausible that the yellow jersey, worn in 1913, would reappear in the first edition of the Tour de France after World War I. And so it did, in 1919, on the shoulders of Christophe.

Philippe Thys, the first three-time Tour de France winner (1913, 1914, 1920)

Desgrange Takes to His Soapbox

Race director Henri Desgrange wanted nothing less than suspense, emotion, and amazing exploits for his race. When the riders didn't meet his expectations, Desgrange didn't mince words.

Philippe Thys, the leader of the Tour from its second stage, let his riding do the talking in the face of Henri Desgrange's criticisms.

Thys wins in Cherbourg on June 29, 1920.

The inventor and organizer of the Tour de France, Henri Desgrange, was also the editorial director of the French sports daily L'Auto. *As an op-ed columnist for his paper, Desgrange could sometimes wield a cruel pen against the riders in his race. His preferred target during the 1920 Tour de France? Belgian racer Philippe Thys . . .*

"Mark my words: I will prove to you that I'm still a capable bike racer. I will win my third Tour de France!" Philippe Thys said in the columns of *L'Auto.* The Belgian two-time Tour winner was retaliating after a venomous op-ed was written by the race director, Henri Desgrange.

The war of words between Desgrange and Thys had been escalating for several days, but it was Desgrange who started the hostilities. Thys, Desgrange wrote in his paper, had lost his edge since last winning the Tour de France in 1914. The interruption of the race during World War I had sapped Thys of his strength. The Belgian would never win another Tour, Desgrange predicted.

The excitement surrounding the 1920 edition of the race was doubled by the verbal fisticuff between Desgrange and Thys. Not to mention that if Thys lived up to his race-winning claims, it would be the Belgian's third triumph—at the time an unprecedented feat in the race's history.

Thys raged into the 1920 race, winning the second stage in Cherbourg before reinforcing his lead in the Pyrenees thanks to solid support from his Belgian team. The Alps produced more of the same: Thys again dominated and rode to the race's finish with more than an hour's advance on his runner-up.

Thys's revenge complete, Desgrange had no choice but to retract his words. That is not to say, however, that the Tour de France boss learned his lesson.

During the same race, French rider Henri Pelissier abandoned the race in anger, convinced that he had been slapped with unwarranted penalties by race director Desgrange. Furious, Desgrange opined that Pelissier didn't know how to suffer on a bike and that the Frenchman would never win a Tour de France. Pelissier won the race three years later.

Desgrange *(left)*, an editorialist with a sometimes razor-sharp pen

I

Italian Passion

The passion of the Italian fans for their national champions could get frighteningly out of hand.

Ottavio Bottecchia, his face caked with dust after winning the Luchon–Perpignan stage on July 4, 1924

In 1924, a renowned French journalist named Albert Londres covered the Tour de France, following the race in a press car for the newspaper *Le Parisien Libéré.* On the July 8 stage between Toulon and Nice, the race took a quick foray into Italy, where hordes of fans clogged the streets. For the first time, an Italian, Ottavio Bottecchia, was in possession of the yellow jersey, making him an instant national hero.

As the legend of the Tour de France grew, so did the passion of the race's fans. So much so that riders often—and justly—feared the enthusiasm of their own supporters.

As the pack rode by, the Italian adulation turned to surprise and then to anger. No yellow jersey was seen in the mix. A group of 20 or so fans manifested their discontent by targeting the car carrying Londres: "Where is Bottecchia? What have you done with our champion?" The journalist escaped unscathed, but only because of police intervention.

In Menton, the scene was the same, the Italian *tifosi* (fans) again menacing Londres with questions: "Where is he?" To save his skin, the journalist could think of only one response: "Bottecchia is dead!" The crowd, bludgeoned by the news, let Londres pass.

At the stage's finish, Londres had just one thought on his mind: To find out what had really happened to Bottecchia. Finally, the journalist found him: The Italian cyclist was dressed in his team's jersey and not the yellow jersey. Bottecchia explained that he had switched his jersey to pass incognito among his fans, fearful that their adulation would cost him time—and possibly the overall race.

Albert Londres during the rest day in Luchon on July 3, 1924

I

Frantz Borrows a Bike

How do you replace a broken bike? Elementary, my dear Frantz

Nicolas Frantz *(seated at right)* and his teammates take advantage of a Tour rest day to fine-tune their equipment.

On July 12, 1928, three days from the finish of that year's Tour de France, Nicolas Frantz was knocking on the door of Tour history. After stealing the yellow jersey on the race's first day, Frantz had yet to lose the lead. And with more than an hour's advance on his nearest rival, the cyclist appeared guaranteed to become the first man to wear the yellow jersey from start to finish in a Tour de France.

Nicolas Frantz's Alcyon team was already savoring victory on the stage linking Metz and Charleville when the fork on Frantz's bicycle snapped in half on a rough stretch of road. Frantz was unhurt, but his bike was destroyed. In 1928, there were no neutral support vehicles carrying spare steeds. Every rider was charged with the upkeep, and the repair if need be, of his bicycle.

At a loss, Frantz saw his chances at the overall race win start to vanish. Fortunately, one of his teammates saw something else: a bike shop, just up the road. The store, however, was far from well stocked. Frantz and his teammates found just one bike for sale . . . a women's model, complete with a headlight and mud guards. To add insult to his ego's injury, Frantz's new bike was three sizes too small.

The yellow jersey didn't have a choice. Frantz set off—his legs folded in half on the small frame—determined to lose as little time as possible. The public watched with astonishment, and sometimes mockery, as Frantz struggled on.

But it was Frantz who got the last laugh, his embarrassment turning to pride at the stage's end in Charleville. The rider from Luxembourg reached the stage's finish with an advantage of 27 minutes on his teammate and runner-up in the overall standings, André Leducq, and kept his precious yellow jersey.

Frantz wore the yellow jersey from the first to last stage of the 1928 Tour.

INSIDE THE TOUR DE FRANCE

CHAPTER 2

Days of Glory

When a champion authors his Tour de France chef d'oeuvre, it's the most charged moment of the race. Spectacular and superhuman—these are exploits we'll remember forever.

2

Leducq Makes His Mark

In 1930, the Tour de France was raced for the first time by national teams, which replaced squads sponsored by advertisers. The new format was a great success, in part thanks to the formidable French team: Charles Pélissier bagged numerous stage wins, and at the foot of the Alps, André Leducq appeared poised to win the overall prize.

Ironically, for André Leducq—winner of the 1930 race—everything fell into place when everything seemed lost.

When it came to descending, no one could match the high-speed abilities of André Leducq. Drawing extra courage from the yellow jersey on his shoulders, Leducq (nicknamed "Dédé") tucked into a vertiginous and tricky descent off the Galibier. Suddenly, at a speed of over 40 miles per hour, he misjudged a corner and tumbled off the road. Dazed, the Frenchman sat on the sidelines before his teammate Pierre Magne helped him to his feet and back onto his bike.

The alarm sounded on the French team. The other national squads, aware that the Tour's race leader was down and possibly out, attacked at the front of the race. For the Italians, in particular, it was a dream opportunity: One of their own, Learco Guerra, was in prime position to usurp the yellow jersey.

Bleeding and half-conscious, Leducq—bolstered by his team—chased onto the opening grades of the Télégraphe climb, where disaster struck again. One of the Frenchman's pedals broke in half, sending him crashing to the tarmac. Convinced that all was lost, Leducq made motions to abandon the race. But with a new pedal and with support of his team, Leducq soldiered on.

Once back on his bike, Leducq amazingly recuperated his wits and strength, powering into the most extraordinary pursuit witnessed in the young history of the Tour de France. Furious at the opportunistic attack by the Italian Guerra, Leducq and the French formation reeled back Guerra just before the finish, and Leducq then won the sprint for the stage.

The French team—Pierre Magne, Marcel Bidot, Jules Merviel, Leducq, Charles Pélissier, and Charles Magne *(left to right)*—pose after a race well won.

A shell-shocked André Leducq after crashing on the descent off the Galibier on July 21, 1930

2

Bartali: Birth of a Champion

Nobody mastered the art of the counterattack like Gino Bartali, blessed with class and Italian elegance.

Gino Bartali attacks the slopes of the Izoard Pass on July 22, 1938, during the stage between Digne and Briançon.

Good Tour de France racers become great Tour de France racers by turning the toughest stages into their own personal stages. Italian rider Gino Bartali was one of the greatest performers in Tour de France history.

W"What's he waiting for? When is he going to attack?" On the opening switchbacks of the Allos climb in the Southern Alps, the Italian journalists were getting fidgety, trying to coax an attack from their precocious young star, Gino Bartali. The Alpine stages of this 1938 Tour de France were already two days old, and Bartali had yet to make even the smallest of moves, preferring to sit at the front of the race and pick off a few mountain-climber points as the summits rolled by.

After an earlier flatland time trial, Bartali was 9 minutes behind the yellow-jersey pace set by the Belgian race leader, Félicien Vervaecke. Bartali, however, appeared unconcerned with his deficit.

His indifference seemed logical. The Italian had won the 1938 Tour of Italy. To then triumph at the Tour de France in the same year was considered by many to be impossible. But Bartali was ready to give it a go.

Without warning, he attacked on the steep grades of the Allos climb. His face, though, kept its same stoic, almost lackadaisical, expression. The only thing Bartali changed was his speed, accelerating away from the rest of the race with astonishing ease. He shed the final stragglers on the slopes of the Izoard and rode to the stage win in Briançon amid manic crowds of Italian fans.

"Don't touch him! He's a god!" the Italian minister of sports reportedly cried at the finish, barring the crowds from swarming over Bartali. The Italian's solitary escape pulled back 17 minutes on the Belgian Vervaecke. Bartali had convincingly stolen the yellow jersey, which he would keep all the way to the race's end in Paris.

On his way to overall victory, the Italian champion solos at the summit of the Allos climb.

2

Bourlon: Art of the Breakaway

Albert Bourlon's breakaway made the Tour de France record book. His mantra for stage success: The early bird gets the worm.

Albert Bourlon launches a solo break from the get-go of the stage between Carcassonne and Luchon on July 11, 1947.

To make their mark, the lesser names in the Tour de France have no choice but to attack. And attack again and again until a prestigious stage win finally comes their way. That was precisely Albert Bourlon's plan. From the first day of the 1947 Tour de France, the Frenchman attacked with stubborn—but unrewarded—persistence.

"Sooner or later, it's going to work," Albert Bourlon repeated to himself throughout the 1947 Tour de France and particularly on July 11, as the Frenchman broke away on yet another solo attack. It was a classic move except for one very important side note: The day's stage—a marathon trek between Carcassonne and Luchon—was less than a mile old. One hundred fifty-seven long miles stretched before the courageous (or perhaps suicidal) Bourlon.

His primary goal, however, was not to launch into an epic solitary escape but to grab an intermediary cash prize arranged for the first rider to reach the town of Espéraza, 31 miles into the race. He easily won the prize in Espéraza, as the peloton opted to save its strength for the two climbs still to come on the stage's menu.

Comfortably off the front, Bourlon shrugged his shoulders and continued with his effort, riding to a 30-minute advantage at Tarascon. Two major climbs—the Port and Portet d'Aspet summits—still loomed ahead, but Bourlon, amazingly, lost nearly none of his lead over the hills.

Strengthened by the growing promise of a stage win, the French rider dug deep into his physical reserves and took an emotional solo victory in Luchon. Unbeknownst to Bourlon, he had also broken two Tour de France records: the longest solo escape in race history (157 miles) and the largest winning margin. When the rest of the race arrived in Luchon, a showered and changed Bourlon had been waiting for 16 minutes and 48 seconds.

Bourlon *(left)* in the company of boxer Marcel Cerdan after riding to victory in Carcassonne

2

Robic: The Accidental Hero

René Vietto or Pierre Brambilla should have won the 1947 Tour de France. But two champions can hide another.

Jean Robic, leading a breakaway on July 20, 1947, between Caen and Paris, claimed the yellow jersey on the race's last stage.

After a forced hiatus during World War II, the Tour de France returned in 1947. The French public clamored for its favorite, René Vietto. But as the stages rolled by, it was another Frenchman, a tenacious pug of a rider from Brittany, who stole the Tour de France show.

Living up to prerace predictions, René Vietto led the 1947 Tour at the exit of the Alps. The consummate teammate during the prewar era, Vietto had countless times sacrificed his own chances to help loft others to victory. With the war now over and the Tour de France back on the map, many thought that Vietto should finally get his just deserts—his turn in the limelight.

Public opinion was so solidly behind Vietto that even the rival West France team refused to help one of its own, the young Jean Robic, achieve his Tour de France dreams. How dare this newcomer, who had never worn the yellow jersey, attack the race leaders. Alone against the world, Robic nonetheless rode a brilliant race, narrowing his overall deficit after a solid showing in the Pyrenees.

Two days before the race's end in Paris—on the occasion of a time trial between Vannes and Saint-Brieuc—"King René" was expected to put the finishing touches on his Tour de France win. Vietto, however, cracked, losing his yellow jersey to a fellow Frenchman, Pierre Brambilla.

Robic, for his part, was still in the hunt, just 2 minutes and 30 seconds behind Brambilla before the Tour's decisive stage, a final haul between Caen and Paris on July 20.

The stage's relatively mountain-free profile didn't appear to cater to attacks, but that didn't stop Robic. Flying away on a rise just outside of Rouen, the Frenchman broke the will of Brambilla. By the finish in Paris, Robic had erased his deficit to win the race. He wore the yellow jersey on only one day in the 1947 Tour, but what a day it was: the last day of the race and for the overall win!

Robic *(center, left)* and Pierre Brambilla *(center, right)*, first and third respectively in the final overall standings

2

Doing the Hugo Hustle

Hugo Koblet's great escape killed his adversaries. But he was in a hurry for more reasons than one.

Hugo Koblet racing through the town of Villeneuve-sur-Lot. The pack is already 3 minutes off his pace.

The most brilliant Tour de France escapes usually occur in the rough-and-tumble terrain of the mountains. But not this one: In arguably the greatest escape in Tour de France history, Hugo Koblet stormed away with jaw-dropping speed on an otherwise mundane transition stage in 1951.

Floating ahead of the pack on a long and lazy downhill, Hugo Koblet looked back to realize that he and Frenchman Louis Déprez had inadvertently bubbled off the front. The duo's advantage was slim, and reason pleaded for them to sit up and wait for the rest of the bunch. Eighty-eight miles of rolling terrain remained in the stage from Brives to Agen. And considering that Koblet was an overall race contender, it was unlikely that the other favorites would allow the Swiss a long breakaway leash.

What was the use of drying up all physical reserves with the Pyrenees looming on the horizon? It was a good question, but one that Koblet didn't ask. The Swiss instead picked up his pace, dropping Déprez and heading out on a solo flyer.

Full of style and grace, Koblet—a sort of James Dean of the peloton—raced at a ferocious tempo but kept an easy, breezy position on the bike. He looked as if he was out for a weekend stroll.

Back in the pack, however, chaos had erupted. Realizing that Koblet could go all the way, the peloton organized into an all-out chase, with the stars of the race grinding away to reel the Swiss in.

But neither Gino Bartali, Louison Bobet, Fausto Coppi, nor Raphaël Geminiani could overhaul Koblet, who hit the stage finish, ran a comb through his hair, and started his stopwatch: Two minutes and 29 seconds was his winning margin.

"If there were two Koblets, I'd change jobs," an admiring Geminiani said at the end of the stage. Bobet, a future three-time Tour de France winner, called Koblet's escape the greatest cycling exploit of the previous decade. But there was an additional reason for Koblet's need for speed: The Swiss was suffering in secret from hemorrhoids. On July 15, 1951, he just wanted to get to the finish—and off his saddle—as fast as possible.

In one of the Tour's mythic breakaways, the Swiss finished 2 minutes and 29 seconds ahead of the pack.

2

Walkowiak from Out of Nowhere

This rider's exploit has become a Tour de France proverb: "The luck of Roger Walkowiak."

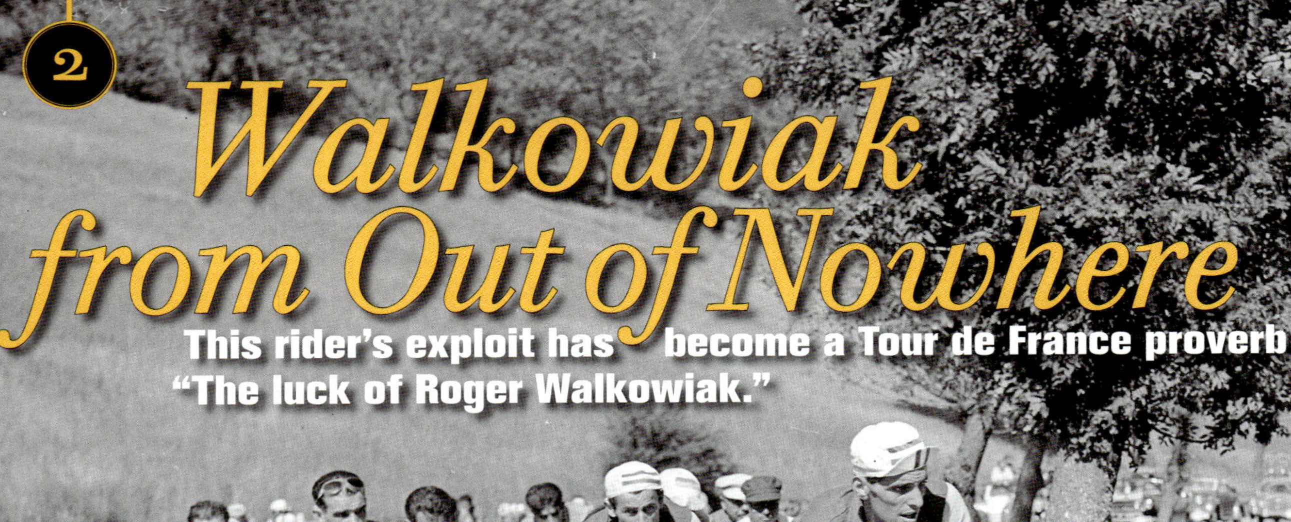

Roger Walkowiak, wearing the yellow jersey, leads the peloton on the stage between Grenoble and Saint-Etienne on July 26, 1956.

"I think Roger has a good chance of winning the Tour de France, but don't tell him that. It would freak him out." Those were the words of Roger Walkowiak's team director during the 1956 Tour de France, a race that was thrown wide open from its very get-go.

Gino Bartali, Fausto Coppi, and Ferdi Kubler, all usual race favorites, forfeited from the start, citing burnout after heavy early-season racing schedules. An injury-hampered Louison Bobet was forced to abandon the Tour, and no single team, it appeared, was strong enough to control the race.

The yellow jersey jumped from rider to rider until the July 11 stage between Lorient and Angers, when a group of 31 unheralded riders took advantage of the apathy of the pack and rode away with the stage, relegating all of the overall favorites to a deficit of more than 18 minutes. At the stage's end, the yellow jersey found its way to Walkowiak, a little-known cyclist on a small regional French team.

As the race wore on, Walkowiak was challenged by just one contender for the yellow-jersey crown, the feisty Charly Gaul, who launched attack after attack in the Alps. Walkowiak, however, managed the mountains with grace, limiting his losses and wearing the yellow jersey all the way home to Paris—without winning a single stage.

The Tour de France is an unpredictable beast. Some years, the race's favorites—beaten by the difficulty of the event or their own lack of aplomb—are unable to live up to their accolades. When the favorites fall, it's a once-in-a-lifetime chance for one of the race's "everymen" to emerge from the woodwork.

Walkowiak *(center)* is congratulated by Yvette Horner after his surprise win at the 1956 Tour.

2

Hinault's Royal Ride

How do you get the best out of Bernard Hinault? By pushing him to his limits.

Bernard Hinault followed by Joop Zoetemelk, second in the overall standings, in a breakaway on Paris's Champs-Elysées

On the morning of July 22, the final stage of the 1979 Tour de France, Bernard Hinault was guaranteed—barring a crash or mechanical mishap—the overall race win. The Frenchman, nicknamed "the Badger" for his tenacious attacking style, wielded a 13-minute advance on his runner-up, Joop Zoetemelk. The Dutchman, however, was feeling frisky and warned Hinault that he would be "shooting from the hip" all day long.

Since 1975, every Tour de France has finished with a majestic flourish on Paris's Champs-Elysées. The stage generally boils down to a mass-sprint fisticuff, allowing a final bow to the speed demons of the race. But from time to time, an opportunistic breakaway can spoil the sprinters' fun.

Zoetemelk kept his word, jumping off the front every chance he got. Hinault, for his part, had nothing to fear from Zoetemelk: He had won a sprint finish the day before and enjoyed an insurmountable lead in the general classification.

The Badger, however, stubborn to the end, made it his personal vendetta to keep close tabs on Zoetemelk, hunting each and every one of the Dutchman's moves. Hinault then took the attacking reins himself, flying away on the morosely named "l'Homme Mort" (Dead Man's) climb. Zoetemelk rejoined Hinault 3 miles later, and the duo continued their cat-and-mouse battle—much to the amusement of the rest of the pack, which assumed the two men would eventually tire and slink back to the bunch.

Think again: Hinault, revved and still ready to race, continued to lead the charge off the front, setting a bullet-train pace all the way to the finish in Paris. Scorching the Champs-Elysées at nearly 40 miles per hour, Hinault edged out Zoetemelk in the finish-line sprint, becoming the first yellow jersey to win the final stage of a Tour de France since 1935.

On July 22, 1979, Hinault crowned his second straight Tour de France triumph with a prestigious stage win on the Champs-Elysées.

2

The Colombian Climbing Revolution

Lucho Herrera, a stunning Colombian climber, became the hero of a whole continent.

Luis "Lucho" Herrera, Beat Breu, Bernard Hinault, and Laurent Fignon *(left to right)*. It's in the company of the race's elite that the little Colombian launched his assault on Alpe d'Huez.

The high-mountain stage between Grenoble and Alpe d'Huez on July 16, 1984, was supposed to be a pyrotechnic showdown between overall race favorites Laurent Fignon and Bernard Hinault. But it was Luis "Lucho" Herrera, a Colombian gardener turned climber, who stole the giants' thunder.

In 1983, the Tour de France hosted for the first time a contingent of climbers from Colombia. The South American mountain men proved their high-hill mettle, but they left the race without a stage win. In 1984, they were back, but things were not yet to go the Colombians' way.

Seeking a first-ever stage win for his country, Luis "Lucho" Herrera twice tried—and twice failed—in the final miles of mountain stages. A talented climber discovered in provincial races in Colombia, Herrera had been a gardener in the town of Fusagasuga before joining the ranks of cycling's elite at the Tour de France.

Herrera knew there was one more mountain prize on the menu of the 1984 Tour: the legendary summit of Alpe d'Huez. The climb, of course, was coveted by every mountain man in the race, and in particular by Bernard Hinault and the yellow-jersey-wearing Laurent Fignon. The two Frenchmen were locked in battle for the race's overall crown.

Hinault launched his hostilities on Alpe d'Huez's opening grades, splintering the pack. Fignon responded with panache, promptly dropping Hinault and accelerating to the summit with just one man on his wheel: Herrera.

With Fignon's goal of controlling Hinault achieved, Herrera launched a final-meters attack to seal the maiden Tour de France stage win for a South American cyclist.

"Calmo! Calmo!" were Herrera's first words at the finish, where the Colombian was swarmed by manic fans. The Colombian press was on the verge of hysteria, and the red-yellow-and-blue flags of Colombia flooded the finish line. "Calmo! Calmo!" Herrera repeated, not yet realizing that he was the new hero of not just his country but of the whole South American continent, as well.

On July 16, 1984, at Alpe d'Huez, Herrera wins a stage of the Tour de France.

2

King of the Mountain

Mont Ventoux—the mountain is mythic. On its slopes, Jean-François Bernard wrote one of the most enthralling stories in the Tour de France book.

Jean-François Bernard attacks the wicked "Giant of Provence."

In the 1987 Tour de France, for the first time since 1958, the race included a mountain time trial to the summit of the daunting Mont Ventoux. In '58, Luxembourgian rider Charly Gaul had taken the honors—and the overall race win. This time around, all eyes were on Colombian climbing god Luis "Lucho" Herrera.

Luis "Lucho" Herrera was regarded as the obvious—and only—favorite for the stage. The harder the mountain, the better the Colombian seemed to ride. And the Ventoux was arguably the hardest climb on the 1987 race route. From the start of the stage, Herrera lived up to his reputation, gobbling the opening grades of the "Giant of Provence" with ease. Hitting the finish with far and away the best time, Herrera—like the rest of the racers—undoubtedly considered the stage won.

Just a handful of riders remained at the time trial's start house, among them Frenchman Jean-François "Jeff" Bernard, a highly touted possible successor to the five-time Tour de France winner, French rider Bernard Hinault.

Jeff ripped through the flatland section leading up to Mont Ventoux on a specially designed aerodynamic time-trial bike, which was a novelty at the time but is common currency today at the Tour de France. At the foot of the Ventoux—and to the astonishment of the crowd—Bernard skidded to a sudden halt. The maneuver, it turned out, was planned, and Bernard exchanged his time-trial bike for a more traditional climbing machine and hauled on toward the finish.

Flirting with oxygen debt, the Frenchman put in the climb of his life, setting the fastest time at every intermediate split and racing to the win a monster 1 minute and 30 seconds faster than the prerace favorite, Herrera.

Bernard Tapie *(left)* congratulates the French rider after his time-trial win on Mont Ventoux on July 2, 1987.

The stage-win ecstasy of Laurent Fignon at Villard-de-Lans

2

Superman!

Laurent Fignon may have been leading the race, but he wasn't happy with his advance. What's a man to do? Attack.

In July 1989, the cycling world was on the edge of its seat. Throughout the three-week Tour de France, the race's yellow jersey juggled back and forth between the shoulders of a former double Tour de France winner, Laurent Fignon, of France, and the American 1986 race winner, Greg LeMond, who was back in the bunch after recovering from a life-threatening hunting accident in 1987.

Dropped by his American rival at Briançon, Fignon reversed his fortunes the next day at Alpe d'Huez, stealing 26 seconds and the yellow jersey from LeMond. However, with three days remaining before the race's end in Paris, the Frenchman considered his lead precarious—particularly knowing that the final day would bring a time trial, a discipline that was LeMond's strongpoint. Fignon had no choice: He had to attack.

Which way would the balance swing in the 1989 Tour de France, the closest contest in the race's history? Frenchman Laurent Fignon, finding a second wind after several stages in difficulty, dropped American Greg LeMond at the summit of Alpe d'Huez, stealing back the yellow jersey. But the Frenchman, not convinced his lead was safe, decided to attack again on the very next stage.

On the mountain roads between Bourg d'Oisans and Villard-de-Lans, Fignon fired off the front, leaving the rest of the race impotent.

Fighting a short but steep ascension to the finish, Fignon was on the verge of exhaustion. Lifted by the cheers of the fans, the Frenchman found a final surge of energy to seal the stage, and the emblazoned logo of his team sponsor, "Super U," on his yellow jersey was looking more and more like "Superman."

"I've taken a big step toward the overall win," Fignon said at the end of the stage. LeMond, relegated to a deficit of 50 seconds, claimed in front of the television cameras to still have "a chance at victory." In private, however, the American reportedly murmured a resigned, "It's over." How wrong he was... (The story continues on page 67.)

Greg LeMond, Pedro Delgado, and Dutch climber Gert-Jan Theunisse try to track down Fignon between Bourg d'Oisans and Villard-de-Lans on July 20, 1989.

2

The Great Escape

Four men with 10 minutes on the peloton. But this isn't your everyday breakaway.

Claudio Chiappucci, Ronan Pensec, Steve Bauer, and Frans Maassen *(left to right)*. The first breakaway of the 1990 Tour de France does its damage.

One year after the holy-moly suspense of the 1989 Tour de France—won by American Greg LeMond by a record 8-second margin—the race was ready for another showdown. LeMond was back, and so was his arch rival, Frenchman Laurent Fignon. The two heroes of the previous edition watched each other with eagle eyes, but they ignored a four-man breakaway that scooted off the front just 4 miles into the race's very first stage.

Steve Bauer, Claudio Chiappucci, Ronan Pensec, and Frans Maassen—the four off the front—made for a dangerous escape. Excluding Maassen, who had limited mountain skills, the other three had a real chance at the race's overall title. Bauer, a Canadian, had finished fourth at the 1988 Tour de France. Chiappucci, an Italian, was the reigning best climber of the Tour of Italy. And Pensec, of France, was well respected as a feisty, all-around talent.

When Chiappucci attacked just 4 miles into the first stage of the 1990 race, the rest of the pack should have taken note. When Bauer, Pensec, and Maassen jumped to join the move, the other race favorites should have sounded the alarm. Instead, the peloton took little interest.

Their reason for not chasing, however, was sound: The morning road stage around the Futuroscope theme park in Poitiers would be followed by a crucial afternoon team time trial. The overall contenders wanted to save their strength.

And so the four men off the front hustled to a lead that reached an insurmountable 13 minutes just 6 miles from the finish. Maassen won the stage in a sprint finish, and Bauer slipped into the yellow jersey. The rest of the racers hung their heads in embarrassment.

"I think we may have made a terrible mistake [in not chasing the breakaway]," Spanish star Pedro Delgado said.

"On the brink of suicide" was the title in the French sports daily *L'Equipe*, hinting that the race favorites had dropped the overall-race ball from the very first stage. Was the 1990 race already won? The answer is on page 69.

The stage to Futuroscope on July 1, 1990, goes to Maassen in a sprint finish.

2

Seigneur: Champion on the Champs-Elysées

The last stage, the most beautiful stage, takes place on the Champs-Elysées. Eddy Seigneur knows how to go out in style.

Eddy Seigneur, drunk with joy, wins on the Champs-Elysées on July 24, 1994.

By 1994, Paris's Champs-Elysées had become the personal stomping ground of Miguel Indurain, the Spaniard on the cusp of sealing his fourth straight victory at the Tour de France. But the French capital's most famous street is also the traditional domain of the race's speed demons, hungry for a final-stage sprint win. In 1994, Frenchman Eddy Seigneur had a very big appetite.

Before the start of the 1994 Tour de France, Eddy Seigneur had promised his family that he would finish the Tour de France—the first in the career of the 23-year-old Frenchman. At the end of the race, just three of the 10 members of the Gan team survived to Paris. Seigneur was one of them. His goal met, the French rider was ready to savor the race's arrival on the Champs-Elysées without any real ambition of winning the stage.

Seigneur, however, revised his stage tactics as the race raged into the French capital. After a relaxed early pace, the peloton went ballistic in Paris, buckling the first of eight laps around the Champs-Elysées at a rocket-launched average speed of 34 miles per hour. At the start of the second lap, a four-man breakaway ditched the front, soon to be joined by none other than Seigneur.

Back in the pack, the sprint teams kept a close eye on the break, never allowing their lead to extend past the 1-minute mark. Despite three weeks of intense racing, Seigneur and the rest of the break appeared to be in fine form. They held off the surging peloton until the final lap, when American Frankie Andreu made a solo move for the win.

The first to react was Seigneur: "Relax, you have the strength to catch Andreu," he told himself. "It's time to attack."

Lifted by the fanatical cheers of the French crowd, Seigneur let his legs do the talking. He caught Andreu some 270 yards from the finish and sprinted on to win the stage. At the 1994 Tour de France, Seigneur had just wanted to make it back to Paris. But never did he dream that he'd be the *first* man back to Paris.

Jean-Marie Leblanc offers a champagne toast to Miguel Indurain, the Spaniard about to win his fourth consecutive Tour de France.

CHAPTER 3

Mountain Duels

Mano a mano. Whether it pits Coppi against Bartali, Anquetil against Poulidor, or Fignon against LeMond, the Tour de France often boils down to a dynamic duel between two champions. Suddenly, the race isn't just about winning. It's also about ego and honor.

3

Coppi and Bartali: The Battle Begins

Fausto Coppi and Gino Bartali—teammates and rivals. And symbols of their time . . .

At the end of a long two-man breakaway between Cannes and Briançon, Fausto Coppi *(in front)* offered the stage victory to his teammate Gino Bartali on Bartali's 35th birthday, July 18, 1949.

The history of the Tour de France is full of dynamic duels—exceptional champions facing off in a fierce fight for the yellow jersey. In 1949, teammates Fausto Coppi and Gino Bartali each had an eye on the overall prize. May the best man win.

It seemed to be a dream team: Fausto Coppi and Gino Bartali united for the first time in the Tour de France. But for their Italian team director Alfredo Binda, it was a delicate tightrope walk between the egos of the two champions.

Coppi begrudgingly agreed to race with Bartali, wary of Bartali's sometimes conniving race strategies. As for Bartali, he didn't take kindly to Coppi's pretensions. The lump sum was an atmosphere of tension and mistrust on the Italian squad.

Things only got worse on the fourth stage of the 1949 race. Coppi, in the midst of an attack with French rider Jacques Marinelli, crashed. The Italian was unhurt, but his bike was beyond repair. Coppi's spare machine was with the Team Italy car, driven by Binda, who remained with the peloton and by Bartali's side instead of racing to Coppi's rescue.

Demoralized, Coppi concluded that his team director had pledged allegiance to Bartali. Coppi entertained thoughts of abandoning the race. It took a colossal effort from his teammates—Bartali included—to convince Coppi to stay in the race.

After the team-car incident, the two Italians watched each other with apprehension. On the eve of the first Alpine stage, Bartali overheard Coppi complain that he was tired and low on morale. With his young teammate struggling, Bartali decided that he found the perfect opportunity to attack: July 18, his 35th birthday.

On the morning of the stage, Bartali, nicknamed "Il Vecchio" (Gino the Old), was stunned to hear Coppi wish him a happy birthday and offer to help him win the day. Throughout the race between Cannes and Briançon, Coppi kept his word, tempering his own desire to attack on the fearsome Izoard climb and instead pacing Bartali to a birthday win. Peace had been achieved between the two Italian champions.

Coppi *(left)* and Bartali *(center)*, teammates and rivals, at the start of the Pau–Luchon stage on July 12, 1949

3

Anquetil and Poulidor: French Favorites

Inseparable and yet so different. Jacques Anquetil and Raymond Poulidor had a rivalry that was the stuff of legends.

On July 12, 1964, in the stage between Brive and Clermont-Ferrand and just 1 kilometer from the summit of the Puy de Dôme, Jacques Anquetil *(left)* and Raymond Poulidor were still battling elbow to elbow.

During the 1964 Tour de France, Jacques Anquetil was the consummate professional, classy and dominating to the end. Raymond Poulidor was the scrappy underdog, capable of moments of mastery that kept the fans in a state of giddy anticipation. Theirs was arguably the greatest duel in Tour history, and it came to a head on the Puy de Dôme climb on July 12, 1964 . . .

At the start of the stage between Andorra and Toulouse, Jacques Anquetil was in the yellow jersey, chasing a record fifth victory at the Tour de France. The tenacious Raymond Poulidor had just won the Tour of Spain. Both men were in peak form, and just 1 minute separated them in the overall standings.

"We avoided looking at each other," Poulidor later said of the duo's *mano a mano* battle to the top of the Puy de Dôme. "We were sure the strain on the other's face would be the mirror image of our own. We had to block out the fatigue and keep fighting."

At first, Poulidor didn't realize that he had dropped Anquetil, who had suddenly hit an oxygen-debt wall. With less than a mile to ride, Poulidor punched to the finish, stealing 42 seconds from Anquetil, who nonetheless succeeded in saving his yellow jersey by a meager 14 seconds.

"If Poulidor had taken the yellow jersey, I would have packed off for home that same night," an exhausted Anquetil said. The Frenchman was still in yellow, however, and could look forward to the Versailles–Paris time trial. The race against the clock was Anquetil's forte, and it would prove to be the key to the Frenchman's fifth Tour de France win.

Poulidor drops Anquetil. He steals 42 seconds in a matter of several hundred meters, but it's not enough to usurp the yellow jersey.

On the top step of the overall podium in Paris, Anquetil leaned over to whisper something in runner-up Poulidor's ear: "You really made me sweat for this one!"

A bunched pack hits the foot of the Puy de Dôme. All the leaders are at the front lines.

3

Merckx Goes It Alone

Act One: Luis Ocana writes a stage-winning chef d'oeuvre. Eddy Merckx is at a loss.

On July 8, 1971, Spaniard Luis Ocana soloed to a stage win in Orcières-Merlette, leaving his great rival, Eddy "the Cannibal" Merckx, of Belgium, 8 minutes and 42 seconds behind.

Called to perform day after day for three weeks, every rider—even the greatest champions—can't help but succumb to the stresses of the Tour de France. After several years of total domination, Eddy Merckx hit an emotional wall in 1971.

Wasted by insomnia, Eddy Merckx (also known as "the Cannibal") was sluggish at the start of the July 8 mountain stage between Grenoble and Orcières-Merlette. He'd already had trouble on the Puy de Dôme several days before after being punched by a spectator, and now the previously indefatigable Merckx was vulnerable prey. Joop Zoetemelk was in yellow, but the real danger was Luis Ocana.

Merckx was put to the test from the get-go of the Grenoble–Orcières-Merlette stage. Off the back on the Laffrey climb, Merckx fought to survive while up front an attacking Ocana—in the midst of the ride of his life—dropped in quick succession Joachim Agostinho, Lucien Van Impe, and finally the yellow-jersey-wearing Zoetemelk.

As for Merckx, his fight for survival would last for 68 miles at the helm of a chase group that was more than happy to let the Cannibal do all the work. Not a single rider would take a pull at the front; all were content to watch Merckx grind himself into the ground.

At the finish, Merckx offered a compliment to stage winner Ocana, who had taken 8 minutes from the Cannibal: "Today, Ocana hammered us. He killed us like El Cordobès [a renowned toreador] kills a bull in the arena."

But Merckx also had a tongue-lashing for the rest of the pack: "No one came to help in the chase—not Thévenet, not Guimard, not Petterson, not Zoetemelk, and all of them had an interest in bringing Ocana back. I could have sat up. I could have forced them to do their share of the work. But what good would that have done? They were only too happy to let me die."

That night, a dejected Cannibal hinted that the Tour, for him, was already over. He had lost. But the next day was a rest day, and as Merckx recovered his racing force, the seed of a counterattack germinated in his mind.

At the stage finish in Orcières-Merlette, the Cannibal is beaten. But has he been beaten for good?

Ocana breaks away, easily distancing rivals Joop Zoetemelk, Joachim Agostinho, and Lucien Van Impe *(left to right)*.

3

The Cannibal on the Hunt

Act Two: The return of Eddy Merckx and the resistance of Luis Ocana. "The Cannibal" never gives up.

On July 10, 1971, after a rest day, Eddy Merckx sets out on a daring attack between Orcières-Merlette and Marseille.

Two days earlier, Spaniard Luis Ocana had made a valiant grab for the yellow jersey, putting on a stunning solo show in the Alpine stage between Grenoble and Orcières-Merlette. Eddy Merckx, for his part, was living a difficult 1971 Tour de France, in trouble every time the road climbed. Many thought the Belgian champion would soon have to accept defeat. The Cannibal, however, had other plans.

The morning after the epic Grenoble–Orcières-Merlette stage won by Luis Ocana, the peloton awoke with heavy legs, taking advantage of the July 9 rest day to nurse their tired limbs. Milling about the recuperating cyclists, the press praised Ocana's yellow-jersey exploits in the Alps but also lauded Eddy Merckx for being gracious in defeat. Secretly, however, the Cannibal was already brewing his revenge.

Merckx was determined to whittle away, second by second, the deficit that separated him from the yellow jersey. The stage that followed the recuperation day was a rolling transition race between the Alps and the Pyrenees. It didn't boast the best topography for an attack, but Merckx didn't care. The Belgian sent his teammate Rinus Wagtmans busting off the front from the start of the stage, launching the hostilities even as Ocana finished a final congratulatory interview in the press caravan. Merckx and six others bubbled up to the attacking Wagtmans, creating a powerful breakaway train steaming off the front.

Back in the bunch, the chase was launched, and Ocana and all the other team leaders set out to reel in the Cannibal. Despite the pack's effort, Merckx personally kept the break alive, motoring at the front of the escape for 153 miles. Seeing his advance drop to 50 seconds, Merckx dug deep and pulled out a final acceleration that paced the break to a 2-minute winning margin in Marseille.

The Mediterranean host city, in fact, had been caught sleeping. Merckx's fury was so fast that the breakaway rolled to the finish line 2 hours earlier than the predicted finish time for the stage!

Out of reach of the yellow jersey, still worn by Luis Ocana, Merckx slips on the race's combined-points leader's jersey in Marseille.

3 Merckx and Ocana: The Luck of the Draw

Act Three: Tragedy strikes. The duel between Eddy Merckx and Luis Ocana takes a Shakespearean turn.

During the Revel–Luchon stage on July 12, 1971, the confidence of Eddy Merckx *(here in yellow in front of his arch rival, Luis Ocana in the early stage of the Tour)* began to give way to doubt.

The common consensus was that Eddy Merckx's day was done. Beaten on the Puy de Dôme and in the Alps, the Cannibal was at the mercy of Luis Ocana, who was untouchable in the mountains of the 1971 Tour de France. But Merckx managed to claw back time—first by captaining a stunning breakaway effort to Marseille and then by winning a time trial in Albi. At the dawn of an epic Pyrenean stage, the Cannibal was again in the overall hunt.

Tensions were growing between Eddy Merckx, of Belgium, and Luis Ocana, of Spain. After the Albi time trial, Merckx suspected that Ocana had benefited from a draft behind a motorbike. Regardless of the claims of dubious conduct, the Cannibal won the stage. Ocana, however, still wore the yellow jersey.

On July 12, the race attacked its first test in the Pyrenees. On the climb to the summit of the Portet d'Aspet, Merckx began to nourish a sneaking suspicion that Ocana might be losing his edge. The two men climbed side by side, bagging summit after summit. On the steep grades of the Mente climb, clouds the color of lead began to shroud the race. At the mountain's summit, the sky split open, flinging rain, hail, and lightning at the peloton.

Ignoring the increasing torrents of rain, Merckx launched into a lunatic descent with Ocana glued to his wheel. The Cannibal narrowly avoided crashing on a washed-out section of road. Ocana wasn't so lucky. As the Spaniard picked himself up, Joop Zoetemelk and Joaquim Agostinho rode into the same trap. Screaming at the top of their lungs, the two riders were unable to warn Ocana in time, as their brakes were rendered useless by the rain. Zoetemelk and Agostinho plowed into the Spaniard at full force.

"I saw myself die," Ocana said later. After lying unconscious in the mud, a spectator's parka covering his body, Ocana was evacuated to the hospital by helicopter.

Merckx, in the meantime, was far up the road, unaware of Ocana's injuries. Later, standing on the stage's podium, Merckx realized that his victory was just the luck of the draw.

"The honor of wearing the yellow jersey belongs to Ocana. I don't have the right to take something that doesn't belong to me," Merckx said.

The Belgian was at the top of the overall standings. But at the start of the next day's stage in Luchon, no yellow jersey was worn.

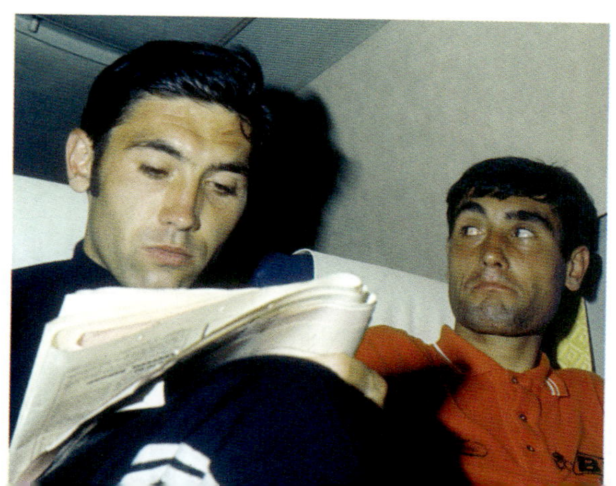

Whether on the roads of the Tour de France or during an air transfer between Marseille and Albi on July 10, 1971, Merckx *(left)* and Ocana were inseparable.

3

On July 10, 1976, between Saint-Gaudens and Saint-Lary-Soulan, race leader Raymond Delisle toils alongside Luis Ocana, Raymond Poulidor, and Joop Zoetemelk *(left to right)*. Lucien Van Impe, at the back of the pack, is preparing his attack...

Guimard Gets Mad

Two champions and a race for the yellow jersey that's too close to call. Here's where the role of team director can make or break the race.

Due to the absence of Eddy Merckx, the doors to the 1976 Tour de France were thrown wide open. Defending champion Bernard Thévenet was in the mix, but the Frenchman didn't appear to be in top form. Many predicted that the overall nod would go to Belgian Lucien Van Impe.

After a turn through the flatlands, the 1976 Tour spiked to an epic mountain battle that featured two of the race's premier climbers: Lucien Van Impe and Dutchman Joop Zoetemelk. The main mountain event was the July 10 hill-heavy race between Saint-Gaudens and Saint-Lary-Soulan. The yellow jersey was up for grabs, as Van Impe and Zoetemelk lingered just seconds behind overall race leader Raymond Delisle, of France.

Van Impe and Zoetemelk watched each other like hawks, matching pedal stroke for pedal stroke in the hills. But for one of them to win, one of them would have to attack. Van Impe's team director, the master tactician Cyril Guimard, knew this better than anyone. At the foot of the Portillon climb—and with the daunting Peyresourde and Pla d'Adet still to come—Guimard gave Van Impe the sign to attack. The Belgian, however, didn't budge.

"Lucien, it's time to attack. Now!" Guimard said, pulling his team car alongside his rider. "Not yet. It's too early," Van Impe replied, worried that he might make himself vulnerable to a counterattack by Zoetemelk. Impatient, Guimard sat back, watching as Van Impe remained glued to Zoetemelk's rhythm. Suddenly, Guimard gunned his car back to within earshot of Van Impe: "I order you to attack! Have I made myself clear?"

Van Impe finally reacted, busting a move and bridging up to Spaniard Luis Ocana, who was already off the front. Zoetemelk's team tried to cajole the Dutchman into accelerating, as well, but Zoetemelk stuck to his tactics. "I still have enough time to counter-attack," he bargained.

Or not: Helped by Ocana, Van Impe hit the finish 3 minutes and 12 seconds faster than Zoetemelk. The Belgian went on to win the '76 Tour de France.

Van Impe, accompanied by Ocana, fights for the stage victory. He wins in Saint-Lary-Soulan, usurping the yellow jersey and dashing the overall hopes of his rivals.

3

Fignon and Hinault: Rabid Rivals

All champions—even the greatest—have their ups and downs.

An ill Laurent Fignon after abandoning the race during the Pau–Superbagnères stage on July 16, 1986

"Merckx? Never heard of him..." Breaking with the traditional gentlemanly manners of the peloton, Frenchman Laurent Fignon had the courage—some would say the audacity—to speak out on other riders, even the greatest of all time. In 1984, on the climb to Alpe d'Huez, Fignon took a verbal hatchet to Bernard Hinault. He probably should have held his tongue.

"When I saw that, I laughed. Really. I was in stitches. His attitude was ridiculous. When you get dropped, the first thing you should do is accept your failure and try to recover," Laurent Fignon said of Bernard Hinault after a 1984 stage to the summit of Alpe d'Huez.

Hinault had been dropped by Fignon and Colombian climber Luis Herrera. But true to his tenacious nature, "the Badger" fought back to the two leaders before launching an attack of his own. It was a suicidal move, and Fignon knew it. The Frenchman sidled back up to Hinault, put the hammer down, and soloed to a stage victory that would lead to his second consecutive Tour de France win.

But no one could forget Fignon's acerbic comments. He had taken to task none other than Hinault, then a four-time Tour de France champion and the undisputed "patron" (boss) of the peloton. The Badger, however, stubborn and proud, didn't say a word.

Fast-forward to 1986. Hinault had won his fifth Tour de France the year before, a race Fignon had sat out due to injury. In the 1986 edition of the race, Hinault hesitated between taking his own shot at victory and helping his young American teammate Greg LeMond to a maiden Tour de France win.

In the stage between Bayonne and Pau on July 15, Hinault made his attacking intentions clear. He single-handedly demolished the pack, attacking solo to steal the yellow jersey.

Fignon, in the meantime, was on the verge of forfeiting the race. And the very next day, the Frenchman did just that. Asked to comment on Fignon's abandonment, Hinault was ready with a potshot of his own: "When I fail, I keep my mouth shut," Hinault said, making reference to his dark day on Alpe d'Huez in 1984. "But I knew I would get my revenge. Today, it's my turn to laugh."

On July 15, 1986, at the end of the Bayonne–Pau stage, Bernard Hinault raced his way into the yellow jersey.

3

LeMond Made to Wait

Greg LeMond will ride in support of Bernard Hinault. The orders are clear—to everyone but LeMond.

On July 17, 1985, the Badger takes a hit on the mountain stage between Toulouse and Luz-Ardiden.

The 1985 Tour de France was a historic opportunity for Bernard Hinault. If the Frenchman won, he would join Jacques Anquetil and Eddy Merckx as the only riders in history to win five Tours de France. But the Badger was in for a rude awakening, the coming of age of one of Hinault's own teammates: American Greg LeMond.

On July 16, at the summit finish at Luz-Ardiden, Bernard Hinault was a thrashed shadow of his usual dominating self. Seeing Hinault pale and gasping for breath, others could easily deduce that his yellow jersey would soon be changing shoulders.

Hinault had been dropped on the stage's ultimate climb by Pedro Delgado and his own La Vie Claire teammate, Greg LeMond. As the two men disappeared up the road, Hinault's shot at history also seemed to vanish before his eyes.

But Hinault's salvation came from his team car. The La Vie Claire squad boss, Paul Koechli, barred LeMond from launching an attack, instead insisting that the American stay put on Delgado's wheel in defense of Hinault's overall race lead.

LeMond accepted his marching orders, and at the stage's end, Hinault kept the yellow jersey. "Greg gave me an enormous helping hand today," a relieved Hinault said after the finish.

LeMond was furious, though. "I blame Koechli!" he said. "He made me lose the Tour de France on a day when I was strong enough to win it."

Hinault rationalized his teammate's reaction. "Greg's feelings are normal for a young, ambitious rider," he said. But it was up to the two men's team owner, Bernard Tapie, to set the record straight and end the conflict.

"If Greg wasn't part of Hinault's team, he'd already be 5 or 6 minutes off the pace. It's Hinault who will win the Tour."

Tour winner Bernard Hinault *(left)* is congratulated by his teammate and runner-up, Greg LeMond, after the final stage of the 1985 race.

3

Eight Seconds

The duel between Greg LeMond and Laurent Fignon held the world in suspense right up to the very last seconds.

On July 23, 1989, Greg LeMond had just one goal for his time trial on the Champs-Elysèes: to make up his 50-second deficit on Laurent Fignon.

In this corner: Laurent Fignon, of France, double Tour de France winner in 1983 and 1984. In the other corner: American Greg LeMond, race champion in 1986 and on the mend after a near-fatal 1987 hunting accident. The final stage of the 1989 edition of the race was a short time trial through the streets of Paris. The day started with Fignon in yellow, ahead by 50 seconds. It ended a little differently.

"Mathematically, LeMond [a strong time-trial performer] should be able to take back 1 second per kilometer on Fignon. [But] if LeMond wants to erase his 50-second deficit, he's going to need to double that," commented Laurent Fignon's team director, Cyril Guimard, before the 1989 Tour's final time trial.

Throughout the 1989 Tour de France, the yellow jersey jumped between Fignon and LeMond. Fignon was fastest in the mountains, but LeMond dominated the time trials. The result was a near stalemate. On the race's last day, Fignon clung to the yellow jersey by 50 seconds. It was a small margin but one deemed sufficient for the overall victory. The distance of the July 23 time trial—just 15.2 miles—was too short for LeMond to hope for a reversal.

The final podium of the 1989 Tour de France: the distress of Fignon and the joy of LeMond

Nobody believed the win was within LeMond's grasp—except LeMond. Fast and furiously, LeMond began his race folded over his aerodynamic triathlete handlebars, then a Tour novelty.

Fignon, the last to hit the course, rolled out 2 minutes later. Suddenly, the crowd buzzed. LeMond was pulling back time; the entire three-week race was about to boil down to a handful of seconds.

LeMond finished in an astounding time; the stage was guaranteed to go to him. But what about the overall race? LeMond, standing on tiptoes, scanned the finishing straight for Fignon. The Frenchman sprinted to the finish 8 seconds too late! The public was in shock, and LeMond was incredulous in the face of his achievement: the narrowest winning margin in Tour history.

3 Chiappucci's Resistance

Claudio Chiappucci versus Greg LeMond. Slowly but surely, the American fought his way back.

Claudio Chiappucci *(right)* and Miguel Indurain between Lourdes and Pau on July 18, 1990. The day before, the Italian saved the yellow jersey by a handful of seconds from American Greg LeMond.

Two weeks earlier, on the first stage of the 1990 Tour de France, four riders had blitzed from the pack, holding the favorites at bay and stealing 10 minutes at the top of the overall standings. The next 14 days of racing, however, took their toll. Canadian Steve Bauer, Frenchman Ronan Pensec, and Dutchman Frans Maassen were now out of the overall hunt. Of the four first-stage escapees, just Claudio Chiappucci remained, clinging desperately to his yellow jersey.

On July 17, at the foot of the Pyrenees, there was no mistaking the day's tactics: American Greg LeMond, the defending race champion, was planning an attack. But when and where on the mountain-riddled stage to Luz-Ardiden would the American make his move? Chiappucci didn't wait for the answer. On the Aspin climb, the Italian launched an effort of his own, breaking free with a small group of 10 riders.

Back in the bunch, the favorites—notably LeMond and Spaniard Pedro Delgado—bided their time, organizing into a steady chase that overhauled the breakaway at the foot of the final ascension. Nine miles from the summit finish at Luz-Ardiden, the yellow-jersey spoils were still free for the taking.

Chiappucci hung in with the favorites, pressing the pace at the front. Was the Italian really as strong as he seemed or was it all just a bluff? To find out, LeMond gunned a series of test accelerations. Chiappucci resisted with panache, riding back to the American's shoulder and looking LeMond in the eyes. The message: "You can't break me. I'm still here."

Fifteen days after shocking the favorites with a surprise attack at Futuroscope, Claudio Chiappucci was still at the forefront of the 1990 Tour de France. On the morning of the giant Pyrenean stage from Blagnac to Luz-Ardiden, the Italian was still wearing yellow. But for how long?

Not for long. In the final mile, LeMond put in an attack that left Chiappucci standing still. But the haggard Italian dug deep into his reserves, somehow finding a final ounce of strength to save his yellow jersey... by a sliver-thin 5-second margin. The 1990 yellow jersey was destined for LeMond, but Chiappucci would at least get to wear it for one more day.

The podium of the 1990 Tour de France: LeMond *(center)* bests Chiappucci *(left)* and Erik Breukink.

R.N
DU TOURMALET

CHAPTER

The Real Men of the Race

Tour de France riders are first and foremost professionals—athletes honed to the tactics and cold strategies of the race. But they are also men, with their strengths and weaknesses, their moments of distress and glory. And maybe that's when they're at their best: when they're at their most human.

4

Gino Bartali, Jean Robic, and Louison Bobet *(right to left)* in the midst of a breakaway between Pau and Saint-Gaudens on July 25, 1950

Comedy of Errors

Gino Bartali played judge and jury, giving his verdict on the 1949 race. But will we ever know the real reason for what he did?

Fighting through torrential rain, Gino Bartali, Jean Robic, and Louison Bobet were neck and neck as they climbed. But with a touch of wheels and the locking of handlebars, the three men crashed to the tarmac. The crowd surged around them—but why?

Trapped in the middle of the mob, Bartali had to wait for race organizers to disperse the crowd so he could ride on, pale and trembling.

Bartali eventually recovered his wits and won the stage in Saint-Gaudens. But his victory speech was a shocker: He announced the departure of the entire Italian team from the race. The Tour's director, Jacques Goddet, hustled to the Italians' hotel to offer his apologies for the fans' behavior. Bartali would hear none of it. "Every day we're pelted by stones, branches, and dirt," he said. "I'm not going to put my life at the mercy of a maniac."

After the end of World War II, embers of aggression still glowed between France and Italy. In 1949, when the Tour made a detour to Val d'Aoste, Italian fans proved to be a menace to French riders. One year later, the French public returned the favor. A storm between France and Italy brewed over the 1950 Tour de France from the very start of the race. On July 25, on the climb up the Aspin, the storm exploded with hurricane force.

But there may have been an ulterior motive for Bartali's decision. He had been beaten the year before by his teammate Fausto Coppi, and this year Bartali was again challenged from inside his own team, this time by Fiorenzo Magni, the new yellow jersey of the race. Bartali assured Magni that he could continue alone (a daunting task without the support of a team). Magni followed Bartali's lead and withdrew from the race with the rest of the Italian contingent.

Fiorenzo Magni *(second from right)* wore the yellow jersey for just one day, July 25, during the 1950 Tour.

4

Feeling Hot, Hot, Hot

The Tour de France can be an oven in July. A rider, broken by the heat, desperately tries to survive.

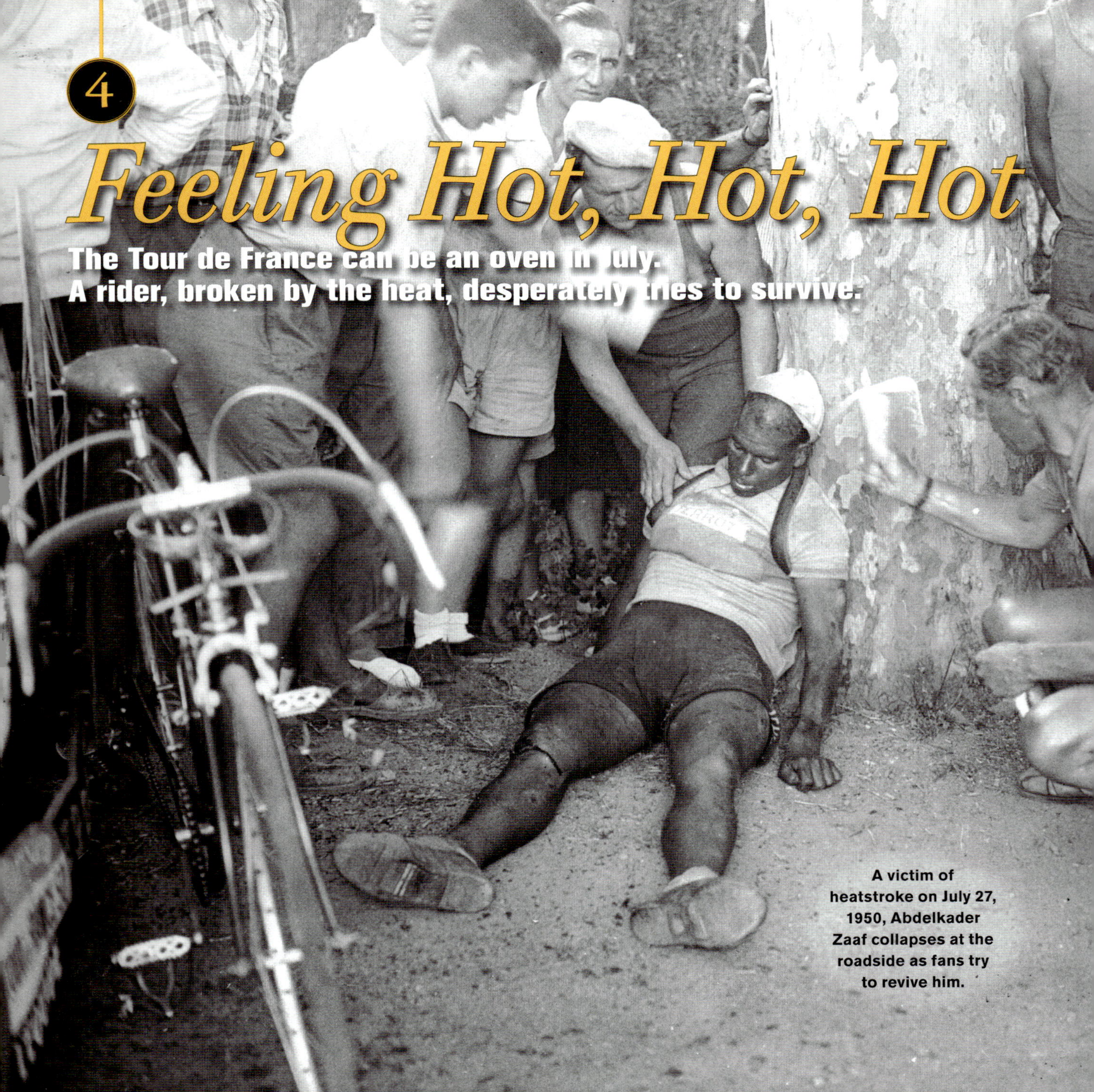

A victim of heatstroke on July 27, 1950, Abdelkader Zaaf collapses at the roadside as fans try to revive him.

The Tour de France is a summer affair, meaning excruciating heat is often added to the race equation. And when temperatures heat up beyond a reasonable degree, the sun can wreak havoc on the race—and the riders, as Abdelkader Zaaf discovered on July 27, 1950.

It was a surreal sight: a rider plagued by hallucinations and riding the wrong way on the 1950 Tour de France stage between Perpignan and Nîmes. Just minutes earlier, he had been sprawled unconscious at the roadside, suffering the effects of heatstroke. Then, suddenly, he came to, remounted his bike, and headed out in a hodgepodge direction. That's when the ambulance found him, bundled him into its care, and whisked him to the hospital.

The Algerian rider would survive, but he would not see his teammate Marcel Molinès win the day's stage in Nîmes. Molinès's victory for the short-lived North African team, in fact, would become a footnote, as race officials and spectators alike were entranced by Abdelkader Zaaf's heatstroke antics.

The fast-spread rumor was that Zaaf had been drunk, that odors of wine had emanated from his pores. Those who knew Zaaf were doubtful. The Algerian, they swore, hardly touched the stuff. The likely truth was that a roadside fan, finding nothing else to ease the heatstroke of the crippled cyclist, doused him with a pitcher of wine.

After regaining his wits at the hospital, Zaaf begged to continue the Tour de France, even suggesting that the ambulance take him back to the place where he had fallen so he wouldn't miss a mile. Race organizers disagreed. Zaaf, lucky to be alive, was inarguably outside the race's allowed time delay.

Zaaf, Hugo Koblet, and Jean Mayen *(left to right)* on the stage between Dijon and Paris on July 27, 1951. The Algerian finished the Tour in an honorable 66th place.

After his heatstroke antics at the 1950 Tour and his show of attacking force between Carcassonne and Montpellier the following year, Zaaf gained star status with the fans.

4

Kubler: The Trash-Talker

When it came to destabilizing the competition, Ferdi Kubler—cycling's original trash-talker—was in a class by himself...

Louison Bobet *(left)* and Ferdi Kubler side by side on the Gap–Briançon stage on August 2, 1950

The NBA isn't the only sports stage where trash-talking can rear its ugly head. Verbally provoking one's opponent to throw him into a state of destabilization is a nasty tactic, but one that sometimes works. Take the 1950 Tour de France as an example . . .

French favorite Louison Bobet finally looked primed for a shot at the overall Tour de France win in 1950. But as the stages went by, Swiss rider Ferdi Kubler stood in his way, usurping the yellow jersey after the 12th stage. Kubler, the race quickly discovered, had an explosive personality. An emotional rider, he was torn by tantrums and would scream at the top of his lungs whenever the racing grew intense. And so it did on the August 2 stage between Gap and Briançon. Bobet attacked for the stage win, and Kubler, exhausted and off the back, babbled stream-of-consciousness insults in his native Swiss German.

That night, Kubler explained himself: "I was screaming to go faster. I need to egg myself on. Bobet's French, so I screamed 'French bastard!' It's good for the morale."

Kubler was still in the yellow jersey on the next day's stage. At the start of the stage, a new mountain test, Kubler rode up alongside Bobet and slapped his own chest Tarzan-style: "Ferdi feeling strong today. And you? Good? I'm going to hurt you later."

Half an hour later, Kubler took another verbal go at Bobet in the opening grades of a climb: "You ready? I'm getting ready to attack . . . Ferdi's feeling fit! You're about to suffer."

Nervous and annoyed, Bobet began to lose his concentration, falling right into the Swiss rider's trap. Kubler made his move, yelling out to Bobet: "Look! Ferdi's a horse!" And with that, he let out a gut-rumbling neighing sound and jumped away on a blistering solo attack. Shocked and in a stupor, Bobet couldn't react, allowing Kubler to gallop off to the overall race win.

Bobet *(left)* savors his stage win in Briançon with Kubler, who maintained his hold on the yellow jersey.

Bobet Meets the Clown

Roger Hassenforder was the class clown of the peloton. Then one day he got serious.

In the 1950s, Roger Hassenforder was cycling's comic. Always quick with a smile and a gag, the Frenchman kept the pack and its fans in good spirits. But when it came to the Tour de France, Hassenforder was dead serious...

On a calm early evening in the French countryside in 1951, a local velodrome hosted a post-Tour track-racing event. Accordion music, candy vendors, the delighted cries of children— nothing was missing from the party atmosphere, not even French great cycling hope Louison Bobet.

Bobet was not yet a three-time Tour de France champion, but he had shown his potential the previous year. In 1951, however, Bobet was off his mark, racing fatigued after a busy early-season campaign that included a win at the Milan–San Remo spring classic.

At the local track that night in August, Bobet, still lacking in cycling punch, was beaten in every event by a young unknown named Hassenforder. The Frenchman, still a boy really, was enlisted in the military but would steal away every chance he got to race his bike. After every competition, Hassenforder would hop on an overnight train with nothing but a tweed suitcase and memories of his races won to keep him company back in the barracks.

In two years' time, however, Hassenforder would become a star of the Tour de France, wearing the yellow jersey for a multiday stint and delighting the crowds with acrobatic stunts such as pedaling his bike backward while sitting on the handlebars.

But that would be in two years. Back at the velodrome, army brat Hassenforder beat Bobet again, flashing a smirking smile at the French professional. Bobet couldn't resist: "I'll see you in the mountains," he called out to Hassenforder, "if, that is, you ever make it to the Tour de France!"

Roger Hassenforder *(far left)* raced his first Tour de France in 1953. He won his first stage two years later, on July 11, 1955, between Metz and Colmar.

Louison Bobet after the La Guerche–Angers time trial on July 10, 1951. The Frenchman finished the Tour in a disappointing 20th place.

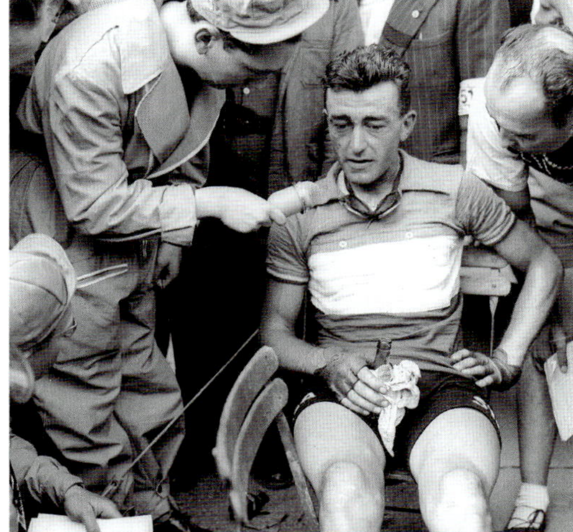

4

"Get away from me! Ferdi is crazy. He's going to explode!"

The Tantrums of Kubler

Ferdi Kubler almost lost everything on Mont Ventoux—including his mind.

A cyclist can be stronger than his adversaries, but he can never be stronger than nature. The mountains and the weather can be a Tour de France rider's biggest competitors. Isn't that right, Mr. Kubler?

"Be careful, Ferdi, the Ventoux is not just any mountain," Raphaël Geminiani warned Swiss rider Ferdi Kubler. The two men were in the midst of a breakaway on July 18, 1955, and about to close in on the ascension of the "Giant of Provence." A formidable French rider, Geminiani was not one to shirk away from a cycling challenge. But the Ventoux was 13.6 miles of agonizing climbing on roads pitched at a leg-breaking 14 percent. To make matters worse, a heat wave was baking the race, and there was not a single spot of shade on the mountain's lunarlike summit.

Kubler, however, turned a deaf ear to Geminiani's warning, blurting back, "I'm not just any rider."

Kubler accelerated away on the opening grades of the Ventoux, quickly finding himself alone at the front of the race. Cooked by the heat, he repeatedly wobbled to a stop, screaming obscenities before gingerly getting on with the climb. The Swiss rider reached the summit and then somehow survived a near-hallucinogenic descent. Kubler's sanity was wilting in the heat.

After stumbling half-conscious into a café for refreshment, Kubler rode on with the race... but in the wrong direction. His team director, Alex Burtin, put him back on track, but minutes later, Kubler cracked, threatening all who tried to approach him.

"Get out of here! Ferdi is crazy. He's going to explode!" Kubler screamed in the third person.

Amazingly, the Swiss rider made it to the end of the stage. Cut by several crashes and sapped by heatstroke, Kubler complained in his bed that night: "The Tour is finished for me. Ferdi's too old. He's in pain!" And with that, Kubler quit cycling.

Ferdi Kubler *(left)* alongside Louison Bobet on the sun-baked route of the 1955 Tour de France

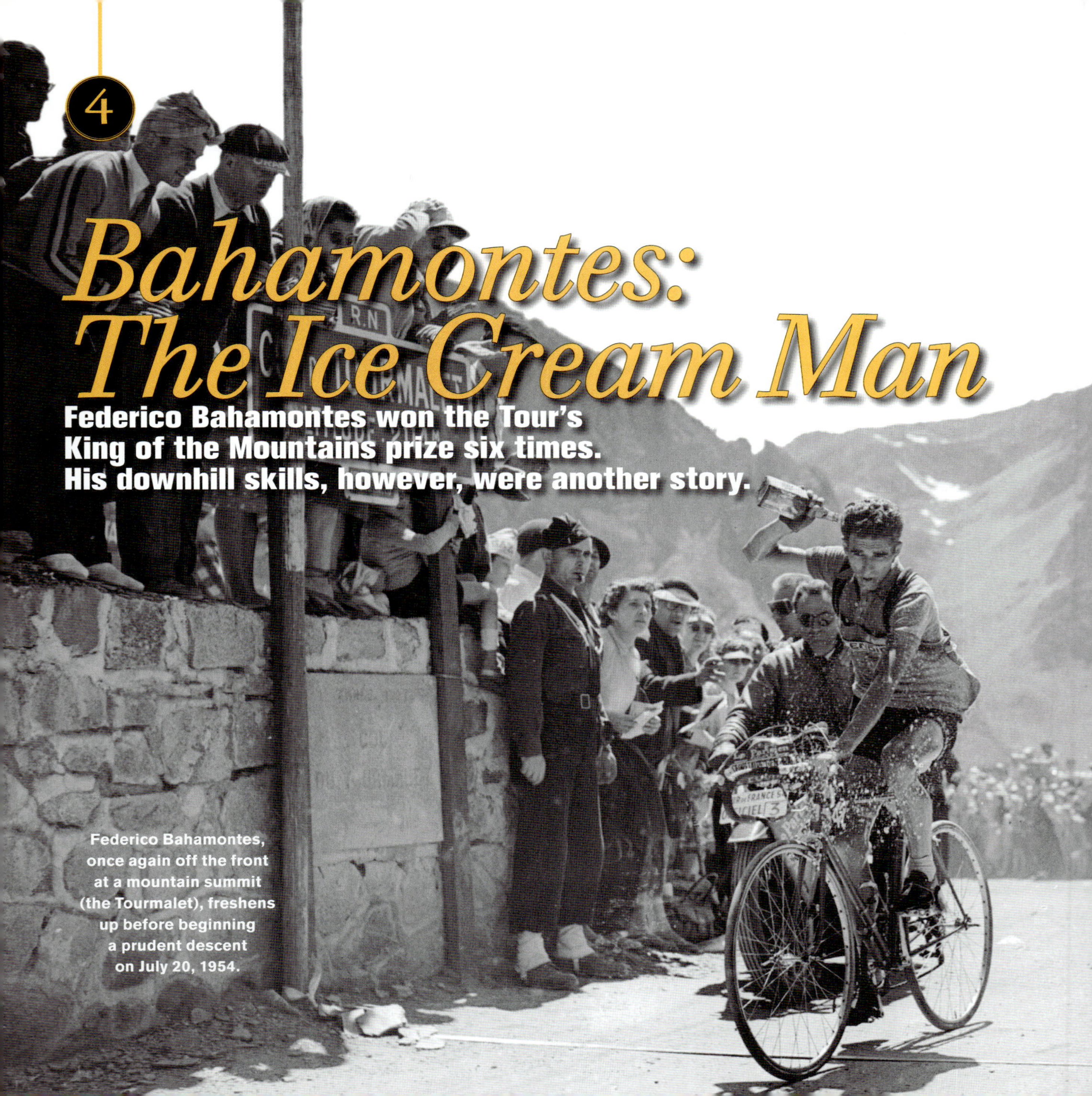

4

Bahamontes: The Ice Cream Man

Federico Bahamontes won the Tour's King of the Mountains prize six times. His downhill skills, however, were another story.

Federico Bahamontes, once again off the front at a mountain summit (the Tourmalet), freshens up before beginning a prudent descent on July 20, 1954.

To win the Tour de France, a rider must be adept in all of the sport's demands: powerful on the flats, quick in the hills, and fearless on the descents. Federico Bahamontes, winner of the Tour de France in 1959, had all of these qualities. Well, at least two out of three...

On July 27, 1954, the Tour de France rolled out for a hill-heavy stage between Grenoble and Briançon. At the top of the day's first obstacle, the Romeyère climb, an ice-cream man had set up his cart. The vendor, however, never thought that one of his customers would be Federico Bahamontes.

The Spanish climbing ace had splintered away from the rest of the pack, racing to a several-minute solo lead. Indifferent to the chase behind, Bahamontes climbed off his bike, sat in the grass, and savored his ice cream. Known as "the Eagle of Toledo" for his climbing grace, Bahamontes was not crazy. He was scared. The Spaniard, you see, loved to climb, but he hated to descend. Bahamontes preferred to downhill in the company of others; it helped him choose his line and control his speed.

And so Bahamontes kept nibbling at his ice cream, and he was just about done when the pack arrived. Jovial to no end, the Spaniard jumped up and joined the fans in spraying the exhausted peloton with cooling water before continuing with the race.

Six times, Bahamontes won the best climber's jersey at the Tour de France. But he won the overall race just once, in 1959. That year, the decisive stage of the race was a time trial that culminated in a summit finish at the Puy de Dôme. It was a perfect stage for Bahamontes: He didn't have to race back down.

On July 13, 1959, at the end of the stage between Saint-Etienne and Grenoble, "the Eagle of Toledo" donned the yellow jersey for the first time in his career. He would keep it all the way to the race's end in Paris.

Caboose

The great race of the '69 Tour wasn't for first, it was for second to last.

Pierre Matignon attacks the peloton, in an effort not to be the "lantern rouge."

Winning the Tour de France is the apotheosis of any cyclist's career. But in reality, most riders are ecstatic with just surviving the Tour from start to finish. There can be only one winner, just as there can be only one last-place finisher. In 1969, the battle not to finish last was just as fierce as the fight for the yellow jersey.

Nineteen sixty-nine was the year of the Cannibal, the first of five Tours de France won by Belgian legend Eddy Merckx. By the sixth stage, Merckx had an ironclad grip on the race, but the battle against becoming the race's "red lantern" (the rider at the caboose of the overall standings) was just beginning.

Two days before the end of the 1969 Tour, two riders were in the running for the red lantern: Frenchmen André Wilhelm and Pierre Matignon, respectively 85th and 86th (and last) in the general classification. Wilhelm, determined not to be the butt of the race, attacked, soloing free on this 20th stage of the race, a 118-mile haul between Brive and Puy de Dôme.

Matignon, for his part, had no intention of keeping his position as the race's caboose. He counterattacked and overhauled Wilhelm—and the rest of the race. Six hours and 40 minutes later, Matignon—against all odds—won the stage 1 minute and 30 seconds ahead of none other than Merckx.

Matignon proves that even the "last-place" rider is capable of greatness.

4

Guimard: Against All Odds

Cyril Guimard: so close and yet so far from his green-jersey dream . . .

On July 23, 1972, on the podium of the Tour de France, race winner Eddy Merckx symbolically offers his green jersey to Cyril Guimard.

For the Tour de France cyclist, the race is a delicate balance between pleasure and pain. French rider Cyril Guimard had more than his fair share of the latter.

A Belgian rider won the final stage of the 1972 Tour de France, but he quickly became an afterthought on July 23 in the Paris suburb of Vincennes. The majority of the race's adulation went to its overall winner: Eddy Merckx.

Merckx's recurrent rival, Luis Ocana, had caught a cold and been fatigued by a strenuous early-season racing program. The Spaniard quickly abandoned the race without ever posting a real challenge. Merckx, on the other hand, was at the summit of his art, and he dominated the three-week race with just one obstacle in his way: Cyril Guimard.

At the start of the Pyrenean stages, Guimard was in the yellow jersey—despite being handicapped by a knee injury. On the 1972 race's rest day in Orcières-Merlette, the knee-crippled Guimard didn't leave his hotel room. And at the next day's stage, the Frenchman had to be carried to the start line on a chair.

Guimard grimaced through the pain, and two days later, he even edged out the great Merckx for a stage win at the top of the Revard climb. By a matter of millimeters, Guimard won the day, usurping at the same time the green jersey awarded to the race's best sprinter.

Guimard, however, was forced to quit the Tour on the penultimate stage of the three-week race. Bludgeoned with knee pain, the Frenchman could survive only 7 miles of the stage linking Vesoul and Auxerre.

On the winners' podium, Merckx made a sign to Guimard, now dressed in civilian clothes and reduced to the role of simple spectator. The Frenchman approached the platform. Merckx shook his hand and offered Guimard, as he broke down in tears, the green sprinter's jersey. Merckx's message was clear: "It's yours. You earned it."

Merckx raises an arm in victory, but it's Guimard *(left)* who eked out the stage win by a matter of millimeters at the summit of Mont Revard on July 18, 1972.

Green-jersey wearer Guimard was forced to abandon the 1972 Tour between Auxerre and Versailles, the race's penultimate stage.

4

Poulidor's Revenge

Raymond Poulidor never won the Tour de France. But he always earned the race's respect...

Perennial Tour de France underdog Raymond Poulidor was on the decline in 1975. At 39 years of age, the Frenchman endured a nightmare race, finishing nearly an hour in back of the yellow jersey. Undaunted, "Poupou" was back in the bunch the following year—for one last hurrah.

In 1975, sentimental French favorite Raymond Poulidor, a victim of bronchitis and age, finished 19th at the Tour de France. "I'll be back next year," he said, adding, "to finish on the podium." Poulidor still believed, but he was likely alone in his optimism: His fans were convinced that the Frenchman had finally ridden one Tour de France too many.

True to his word, Poulidor was ready and waiting at the start of the 1976 race, announcing that, at 40, he would be making his last Tour de France appearance. That year the race was a climber's paradise. Lucien Van Impe, of Belgium, and Dutchman Joop Zoetemelk waged war in the Pyrenees and would finish first and second respectively on the overall podium. The battle for third, however—featuring Poulidor and Frenchman Raymond Delisle—was just as fierce.

The third-place match reached its climax on July 16 during the 20th stage. Bolstered by his fan base, the ever-popular Poulidor jumped away from Delisle on the climb to the summit of the Puy de Dôme, stealing 30 seconds from his fellow Frenchman on the stage.

On the race's last day—an individual time trial on the Champs-Elysées—"Poupou" put in an inspired ride, closing his Tour de France book with a 9-second advance on the hard-charging Delisle. At 40 years old, Poulidor was again on the podium of the Tour de France. He had made it there for the eighth time in his career—without ever winning the race.

Luis Ocana *(left)* and Joop Zoetemelk *(second from left)* were two of the principal protagonists of the 1976 Tour de France. But the French public was rapt in the duel between Raymond Delisle *(in the yellow jersey)* and old man Raymond Poulidor *(in the blue jersey in back).*

Left to right: Zoetemelk (second place), Lucien Van Impe (first), Michel Pollentier (seventh), Ocana (14th), and Poulidor (third) on the Champs-Elysées on July 18, 1976

4

Agostinho: The Cattle Caller

One day, Joachim Agostinho was forced to choose between the loves of his life: the Tour de France and his cattle herd back home in Portugal.

Portuguese climber Joachim Agostinho reached the podium of the Tour de France for the first time at age 36, finishing third overall in 1978. The following year, he wanted to repeat his exploit. The only problem? The cows didn't come home.

Joachim Agostinho caught the Tour de France's attention from his very first participation in 1969. Light, energetic, and with an innate sense of tactics, the Portuguese rider was a born climber. But any prize money Agostinho won while racing his bike went to funding his other passions: his farm back home and particularly his herd of cattle.

In 1979, just days before the start of the Tour de France, Agostinho's herd vanished overnight; the Portuguese had been victimized by cattle rustlers. The ensuing choice was agonizing: Should he abandon his cash cows for his beloved Tour de France or abandon the Tour de France for his beloved cows? Neither, Agostinho decided.

Shelving his final race preparations, Agostinho trekked out alone through the hills of his native Estrémadure region of Portugal. Tipped off by witnesses, Agostinho located his cattle and wrangled them home. With nary a second to spare, he then hustled to Paris to make the June 27 prologue of the Tour de France. Three days later, Agostinho finished second on a rough mountain haul from Luchon to Superbagnères. The winner later in the race on the summit of Alpe d'Huez, Agostinho got his goal: a third-place overall finish.

The Portuguese was pleased with his finish, but his fans couldn't help but wonder where he might have placed had he not gone cattle calling just days before the race. Legend has it that Agostinho plodded some 50 exhausting miles on foot to bring his cows home.

Attacking solo, Agostinho flies free for the most prestigious of stage wins in the Tour de France.

4

Paging Mr. Delgado

Pedro Delgado was the defending Tour de France champion. Everybody was waiting for him . . . and waiting . . . and waiting.

Spaniard Pedro Delgado, winner of the 1988 Tour de France– and loser in the Luxembourg prologue on July 1, 1989!

The 1989 Tour de France kicked off with a prologue time trial in Luxembourg on July 1. The list of heavyweight race favorites included American Greg LeMond, Frenchman Laurent Fignon, and, of course, defending champion Pedro Delgado, of Spain. Delgado, however, was nearly a no-show.

The previous year's Tour de France champion is traditionally the guest of honor at the following year's prologue. With the yellow jersey on his shoulders, the reigning Tour king is the last to roll from the start house. With nearly 200 riders in the race, Pedro Delgado, the 1989 defending champ and the last to ride, could bide his time. His start wasn't scheduled until 5:17 in the afternoon.

At 4:00, Delgado left his hotel and climbed onto his bike to pedal the short 3-mile distance to the race start in downtown Luxembourg. Easy and breezy while warming up, Delgado was all smiles, stopping repeatedly to sign autographs and shake hands with his fans. After a quick trip to his Reynolds team bus, "Perico" sauntered over to the prologue's sign-in table.

One hour had passed, but about 15 minutes still remained for Delgado's team directors to review his plan of attack for the time trial. His team, however, was at a loss. Delgado was nowhere to be found.

The Spaniard's start time came . . . and went. The race and the crowd were in a daze, and the hypothesis of a kidnapping by the Basque separatist group ETA was even bandied about. Finally, Delgado surged to the start house, frantically clipped into his pedals, and sprinted onto the course–2 minutes and 40 seconds late.

Finishing in last place in the prologue, the defending champion became the first caboose of the 1989 race.

On July 10, 1989, between Pau and Cauterets, Delgado tries to make up for lost time. But the stage would be won by one Miguel Indurain.

4

Hamilton: The Masochist

His collarbone broken, Hamilton lets his heart and legs do the talking.

At the 2003 edition of the Tour de France, Tyler Hamilton rode the majority of the race with a broken collarbone. A mass crash in the race's first stage was all it took to stack the cards against the American cyclist. But Hamilton's will and tolerance for pain were unbreakable.

Etched into the collective memory of the 2003 Tour de France is the image of an injured Tyler Hamilton, his face a mask of pain, fighting to survive a mountainous 16th stage. Just 9 miles into the race, a breakaway of 14 riders bubbled off the front. Hamilton was not among the 14, but sensing that this break had the potential to go all the way, the American pulled away from the pack. Keeping his broken shoulder as immobile as possible, Hamilton bridged up to the break.

Natural selection predicts that the weak and hurt should be shed off the back. But Hamilton bucked the odds and attacked, gritting away his pain and embarking on a 57-mile solo adventure.

The peloton, while stupefied by Hamilton's audacity, was not concerned. A man with a cracked collarbone simply couldn't survive to the finish. Hamilton's CSC team director, Bjarne Riis, had other ideas. The 1996 Tour champion galvanized his rider, cajoling the American to ride the race of his life.

The pack ratcheted into an all-out chase, but Hamilton held them off. Fighting a headwind and a broken body, the American somehow hit the finish first, sealing his maiden Tour de France stage win and climbing to a formidable sixth in the general classification.

Hamilton attacks the peloton, which is left in awe.

After riding in pain for two weeks, victory was especially sweet.

5

Anquetil against All

Jacques Anquetil had already pocketed a Tour de France. But then just "winning" wasn't enough. It was time to dominate.

June 25, 1961, the first day of the Tour de France: After instigating the winning breakaway in the morning's half stage, Jacques Anquetil won the afternoon's time trial in Versailles to take the yellow jersey. He never gave it back.

In 1961, Jacques Anquetil didn't mince words: Four years after his triumph in 1957, the Frenchman was back to win the Tour de France "with panache."

From the first day of the 1961 Tour de France and his untouchable performance in the opening time trial in Versailles, Jacques Anquetil was the logical favorite for the overall title. His French team, however, soon found itself the target of a flurry of attacks—from the other teams, who sought out cracks in the squad's armor, but also from the press, who considered the French formation too dominating.

Forced to police the peloton for leader Anquetil, the French team tirelessly monitored every move that bubbled off the front. On July 1, a breakaway charged off the front on the roads between Belfort and Chalon-sur-Saône. French team riders Joseph Groussard and Jean Stablinski bridged up to keep an eye on the break, but the rest of the race—Anquetil included—was soon 17 minutes adrift.

"We're here to win the race, not to put on a show," French national team director Marcel Bidot had said just the night before, shunting the glamorous light his star-studded team shed on the Tour de France. Bidot's priority was to guarantee that Anquetil brought the yellow jersey back to Paris. To that end, Bidot asked his team leader if Groussard and Stablinski should be given the order to break the rhythm of the escape so that Anquetil would have a chance at latching back on.

Anquetil had different ideas. For him, you could calculate strategies until the cows came home. That wasn't how he wanted to win the race ("with panache"). And so Anquetil took the reins of the peloton himself. A one-man locomotive, the Frenchman captained the front of the bunch, ignoring a feed zone and attacking without an ounce of help from other riders. For 20 miles, Anquetil pushed a furious pace. The rest of the pack was strung out in single-file agony, and slowly but surely, Anquetil reeled the break back. Opinion was now unanimous: With or without the powerful French team, Anquetil was the strongest man in the race.

At the 1961 Tour de France, there was Anquetil... and then the rest (here between Luchon and Pau on July 11).

"We're here to win the race, not to put on a show," said Marcel Bidot. On the rest day in Montpellier on July 8, Anquetil proves his team director wrong.

5

Anquetil Drowned in Doubt

It's the mark of true champions: When ravaged by doubt, they find a way to emerge greater than ever.

Dropped on the Andorra–Toulouse stage on July 6, 1964, Jacques Anquetil struggles to follow his teammate Louis Rostollan.

"Of all the racers I have known, he was the most courageous," team director Raphaël Geminiani said of his star rider, Frenchman Jacques Anquetil. But even a champion of Anquetil's ilk could be devoured by doubt . . .

On the opening grades of the Envalira climb—just minutes into a stage of the 1964 Tour de France—Jacques Anquetil was already off the back. Raymond Poulidor and Federico Bahamontes had danced away from the Frenchman, leaving Anquetil lagging with just teammate Louis Rostollan at his side for moral support.

Already a four-time Tour de France champion, Anquetil had thought long and hard before starting the 1964 race. Perennial number two Raymond Poulidor had become a favorite of the fans, some of whom were bored with Anquetil's dominating ways. But there was also a prediction, written by a supposed clairvoyant named Belline in a major daily paper, that had said that Anquetil would "disappear" on the race's 14th stage, July 6, near Andorra. In French, "disappear" could have two contexts: to abandon the race, or to die. From the start of the Tour, Anquetil couldn't forget the malediction, allowing his strength to be sapped by worry.

To coax Anquetil out of his funk, Geminiani had taken him to the Radio Andorra party thrown on the race's rest day. Anquetil was known for his penchant for parties, but on this occasion, the Frenchman remained preoccupied and quiet.

And on the Envalira climb, with Poulidor and Bahamontes far in front, Anquetil considered abandoning the race. At the summit, he was 5 minutes off the pace. Geminiani pulled up alongside Anquetil and screamed, "Jacques, if you're going to die, at least do it at the front of the race, not in the broom wagon at the back of the bunch!"

Anquetil smiled, and lo and behold, the curse was broken. The Frenchman flew into the descent with so much abandon that it was Geminiani's turn to get scared. Toward the stage's finish in Toulouse, Anquetil rejoined the front of the race and even stole a few seconds from Poulidor—who was cursed in turn with a flat tire with the finish line in sight.

Anquetil *(right)* with his team director, Raphaël Geminiani, before the start of the 1964 Tour

5

The Birth of the Cannibal

He's arguably the greatest rider in the history of cycling.

Brimming with confidence, Eddy Merckx is determined to show his supremacy during his very first Tour de France participation.

In 1969, man walked on the moon. But it was also the year that Belgian Eddy Merckx first rode in the Tour de France. The rest, as they say, is history.

"On every stage, he puts our heads under a guillotine," Raymond Poulidor said during the 1969 race, overwhelmed by the crushing superiority of Eddy Merckx. That year, just one man could have stood between Merckx and overall victory: the Tour's doctor, who on his prerace rider examinations detected a small anomaly on the Belgian's electrocardiogram. The diagnosis was a slightly irregular heartbeat. The verdict? Nothing serious. Merckx could race.

Merckx launched his first attack on the Ballon d'Alsace climb on the race's sixth stage. "I wanted to see how I stacked up against the others," he said later. Nineteen sixty-nine, remember, was Merckx's first Tour de France attempt. Just a handful of riders was able to grab the Belgian's wheel. Favorites such as Poulidor and Felice Gimondi sunk off the back, conveniently citing excuses of "mechanical mishap" and "flat tire" respectively. Merckx earned his first Tour stage win. He would earn six more in 1969, including the race's three time trials and a fabulous mountain performance between Luchon and Mourenx in the Pyrenees.

For Merckx, it was almost too easy to seal Belgium's first Tour triumph since Sylvère Maës's 30 years earlier. Merckx's Faema team was still intact at the race's end in Paris, and in addition to the yellow jersey, the Belgian had won the green sprinter's jersey as well as the King of the Mountains prize.

A few days before the end of the race, Christian Raymond, a corporate representative on the rival Peugeot team, was visited by his daughter. Teasingly, she said to her father, "This Belgian guy—he doesn't even leave you the crumbs. He's a real cannibal..."

Merckx, his Faema squad, and team director Guillaume Driessens salute the crowd after their victory at the 1969 Tour.

In 1969, Merckx won every possible jersey and a nickname: the Cannibal.

On July 15, 1975, at the start of the stage between Valloire and Morzine-Avoriaz, Eddy Merckx crashed and fractured his jaw.

Jaw Breaker

Eddy Merckx would never admit to being beaten. Just another reason why he almost always won.

For the first time in its history, the Tour de France finished on Paris's Champs-Elysées in 1975. Cycling fans came from the world over, expecting to herald the sixth win of the majestic Eddy Merckx. Instead, Merckx finished second, beaten by the scrappy and persistent attacks of Frenchman Bernard Thévenet.

And yet, on the race's podium in Paris, French president Valéry Giscard d'Estaing paid his greatest compliments to Merckx: "I have a lot of respect for the courage you showed during this race. There will be other Tours de France where you will undoubtedly seize a record sixth win."

Merckx would never win a sixth Tour de France—a record that might have been his in 1975 had it not been for Lady Bad Luck. After being punched in the gut by a lunatic fan on the climb up the Puy de Dôme, Merckx became the victim of a new incident on July 15. Before the start of the stage linking Valloire and Morzine-Avoriaz, the Belgian suffered a heavy crash. The diagnosis was grim: In addition to having contusions on his hip and knee, Merckx had fractured his jaw. His doctor, fearing that the injury could lead to respiratory trouble, forbade Merckx from continuing with the race.

In 1975, Eddy Merckx was on the cusp of winning a record sixth Tour de France. But there's much more to the legend of the Cannibal than just his victories.

Merckx had nothing to prove. Already a five-time Tour winner, he could have walked away with his head held high. Instead, the Belgian carried on with the race. Though he could barely eat in the feed zones and his breathing was labored and painful, Merckx somehow completed the world's toughest bike race—and in second place, no less.

French president Valéry Giscard d'Estaing *(center)* with 1975 Tour de France winner Bernard Thévenet *(left)* and runner-up Merckx

5

Hinault: Judge and Jury

When a rider shows a little too much gumption, it's up to the yellow jersey to put him back in his place.

Bernard Vallet *(right)* with Beat Breu on July 22, 1982, in Morzine

In 1982, the 69th edition of the Tour de France offered a fourth career win to Bernard Hinault. The Frenchman also won the Tour of Italy that same year. But Hinault wasn't just a major tour champion. He was also the respected "patron" (boss) of the peloton. And when the boss talks, you'd better listen.

The 1982 Tour de France didn't offer much in the way of suspense. Bernard Hinault had a stranglehold on the race from its start. Halfway through the race, it was clear that the yellow jersey wouldn't be leaving the Frenchman's shoulders. As for the polka-dot top climber's prize, that jersey, too, appeared to be wrapped up by a Bernard: Bernard Vallet.

On the Tour's 18th stage, just a few days from the end of the race in Paris, Vallet crashed. Another climber in the race, Beat Breu, of Switzerland, suddenly saw his window of opportunity. He jumped off the front, hoping at the day's end to steal the polka-dot jersey from Vallet, of France. Hinault, a staunch defender of pack etiquette, was furious: Thou shalt not attack a rider who hath crashed.

As the peloton slowed its pace to wait for Vallet, Hinault bridged up to the attacking Breu and scolded, "Listen up. You don't attack a man when he's down, especially when it's one of the leaders of the race. Cut the crap right now. The Tour de France is over. If you're really this strong, you should have shown it sooner!"

The shamed Breu promptly cut his effort, allowing the peloton to gobble him back. Four days later, on July 25, Vallet rode home to Paris as the race's mountain king.

Vallet, Raymond Martin, Joop Zoetemelk, Robert Alban, and Bernard Hinault *(left to right)* in pursuit of Beat Breu between Pau and Saint-Lary-Soulan on July 17, 1982. They won't succeed in hunting Breu down, but Vallet will keep the polka-dot jersey until the race's end in Paris.

5

On July 25, 1982, Bernard Hinault wins the final-stage sprint on the Champs-Elysées in front of Adrie Van Der Poel *(left)* and the entire peloton.

Lack of Panache

"He lacks panache." There's nothing better—or further from the truth—to raise the ire of Bernard Hinault.

P

"Panache? Not important. I'm here to win the yellow jersey. That's it," an irritated Bernard Hinault said when questioned about his supposed lack of racing spark. In 1982, the Frenchman again put the Tour de France in a vise grip. Winner of the prologue, Hinault then proceeded to pitch the climbers abysmally off the pace in the race's remaining time trials. Halfway home to Paris, his nearest rival, Joop Zoetemelk, was already resigned to second.

Like Jacques Anquetil and Eddy Merckx before him, Bernard Hinault had a problem: It wasn't always easy to find an apt Tour de France adversary. In the eyes of the public, his wins came too easily. The Frenchman was sometimes criticized for lacking panache. We'll see about that, Hinault answered.

The race's fans felt cheated by a Tour that lacked suspense. Hinault, however, had been a punchy force all race long. He competed in the bonus sprints and attacked with verve on the rough-and-tumble cobblestones in the north of France. The bottom line was that Hinault was just a victim of his own racing superiority.

Two days before the race's end on July 25 in Paris, Hinault devised a plan to up his panache factor. "I want to try to win on the Champs-Elysées," he told his flabbergasted teammates.

On the second circuit lap on the French capital's most famous street, Hinault attacked. But the pack would have none of it and squelched all breaks to set up an inevitable mass-sprint finish.

With less than a mile to go, Hinault was still lurking at the back of the bunch. Glued to the wheel of his teammate Charly Bérard, the yellow jersey began to inch toward the front. One by one, Hinault passed his rivals before putting in a final burst of speed to steal the stage (with panache!) right under the noses of the world's best sprinters.

Hinault is congratulated by the then Paris mayor, Jacques Chirac, after winning the 1982 Tour de France, his fourth overall success.

5

Bernard Hinault courageously completes the July 13, 1985, stage between Autrans and Saint-Etienne despite a broken nose.

Hinault: Nose for Problems

All that matters is overall victory—at any cost.

On July 13, 1985, the peloton oscillated in chaos in the lead-up to a mass-sprint finish in Saint-Etienne. Approximately one-quarter of a mile from the line, a crash exploded near the front of the bunch. As the victims picked themselves up, one remained splayed at the roadside: the yellow-jersey-wearing Bernard Hinault. The Frenchman's head had been run over, and his face was half-obscured by blood.

"When I touched my face, I realized I was gushing blood. There was so much, I was blinded," Hinault said later. The then four-time race champion delicately climbed onto his bike and pedaled the short distance to the finish before being evacuated to the hospital. The diagnosis: a double fracture of his nose.

Despite the pain, Hinault kept his sense of humor. "Oh well, in the worst-case scenario, it'll be [my teammate] Greg LeMond who wins the Tour," he joked.

The next day, the Tour confronted a difficult stage to Aurillac, navigating several daunting Massif Central climbs in atrocious heat. The entire world watched Hinault, waiting to see if the Frenchman would cave to the pain.

Throughout the stage, however, Hinault didn't show the slightest hint of emotion. Just a day after his terrifying crash, the Frenchman finished the stage without losing a single second to his adversaries.

"Believe me—the old man's not dead!" Hinault had warned before the stage's start.

From start to finish, the Tour de France is a procession of risks. No rider is out of harm's way—not even the yellow jersey. Case in point: Frenchman Bernard Hinault was on the warpath to Tour win number five in 1985 when disaster walked his way.

At 31—and with a broken nose—Hinault joined Jacques Anquetil and Eddy Merckx as the only five-time winners of the Tour de France.

Tour doctors treat Hinault, the victim of a spectacular crash 400 yards from the stage finish in Saint-Etienne.

5

Indurain Takes His Turn

At the top of the Pyrenees, Miguel Indurain found a yellow jersey. A new cycling era was about to begin...

Claudio Chiappucci *(left)* and Miguel Indurain battle side by side on the stage between Jaca and Val-Louron.

Compared with previous editions of the race, the 1991 Tour de France was light on the mountains. Therefore the climbing stages that did punctuate the route were all the more crucial—particularly the one on July 19, a five-summit Pyrenean haul ending with a final climb to the finish at Val-Louron. The first of the mountain beasts encountered was the Tourmalet. Triple race winner Greg LeMond launched the hostilities, but his move was squelched and then countered by Claudio Chiappucci, otherwise known as "the Devil."

Dropped on the final switchbacks before the Tourmalet's summit, LeMond blitzed a death-defying descent to regain contact with the lead group. To the American's surprise, however, one rider was missing from the front of the race: Miguel Indurain, a lieutenant to Pedro Delgado on the Spanish Banesto team.

When Chiappucci jumped to take up the chase, neither LeMond nor the race's current yellow jersey, Frenchman Luc Leblanc, could follow. On the Aspin climb, Indurain and Chiappucci raged farther into the lead amid a rabid collection of cheering fans. At the stage's finish, Chiappucci outsprinted Indurain for the stage honors. But the big Spaniard received a very satisfactory consolation prize: the first yellow jersey of his career.

As Chiappucci paid a poststage visit to the press, LeMond trailed into the finish 7 minutes off the pace. The American's overall hopes were more or less dead. "Nothing can be done for him [LeMond]," Chiappucci said. "Indurain is the strongest of us all."

The capital stage of the 1991 Tour de France was a mountain haul between Jaca, Spain, and Val-Louron, France. With the yellow jersey on the line, Spaniard Miguel Indurain attacked with the flamboyant Italian Claudio Chiappucci. As for defending champion Greg LeMond, the American's Tour de France goose appeared to be cooked.

On July 19, 1991, American Greg LeMond *(left)* is dropped by the group of race favorites.

5

Brotherly Love

On his bike, the champion has a one-track mind. He's riding for glory.

On July 12, 1993, Prudencio Indurain battles bad weather in the Madine Lake time trial.

In 1993, the Tour de France was a family affair for race favorite Miguel Indurain. The future five-time winner was joined on his Banesto team by his brother Prudencio, who was making his Tour de France debut. Prudencio, however, was almost shown an early exit, thanks to his brother.

For the first time, Prudencio Indurain and his big brother Miguel rode together at the Tour de France. They bunked together at the Banesto team's hotels, and when they emerged in the morning, it was difficult to tell which brother was which. With the same build, the same size, and the same smile, the Indurain boys could almost pass for twins. But the similarities ended with their personalities: Miguel's timidity and reserve contrasted with his little brother's gregarious nature.

At the start of the July 12 individual time trial around Lake Madine, the course was ripped by wind and plastered with glacial hail and rain. The first riders out of the start house didn't really race. They tried to survive. Prudencio was among them, and he finished in a disastrous time.

Several hours later, Miguel took his turn at the start ramp. The time-trial specialist, unaware of his brother's earlier tribulations, raged through the course, racing toward an almost certain stage victory—a win that had the potential to send Prudencio back to the family farm in Villava, Spain.

If Miguel kept his torrid pace all the way to the finish, he would push Prudencio out of the time delay established by the race's organizers, meaning Prudencio would be disqualified from continuing the Tour. "Unless the hand of God decides otherwise," the Banesto team director, José Miguel Echavarri, would say later.

Five miles from the finish line, Miguel Indurain's rocket race was stalled by a flat tire, which caused the Spanish giant to forfeit time. But how much?

At the end of the day, Miguel was first on the stage's classification. Prudencio was last—but saved from race elimination by 24 seconds!

"I'm glad I got that flat," Miguel said. Prudencio, relieved, had this to say: "Today I can take pride in the fact that my performance was just as bad as Miguel's was good."

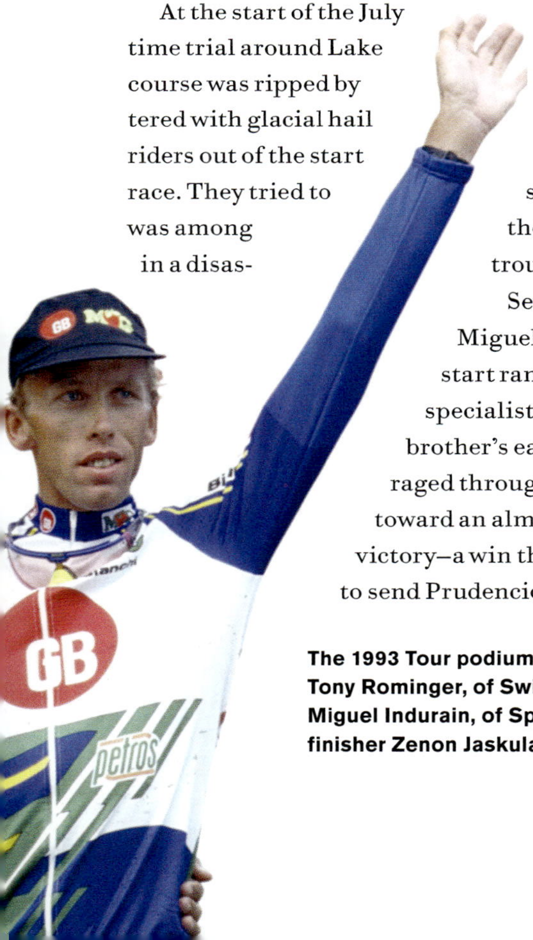

The 1993 Tour podium *(from left)*: Runner-up Tony Rominger, of Switzerland, champion Miguel Indurain, of Spain, and third-place finisher Zenon Jaskula, of Poland

5

Indurain: The End

King Miguel's star is fading.
Every champion will have to face his day of defeat.

Manuel Fernandez Gines, Abraham Olano, and Miguel Indurain–the deposed king–watch as a rider escapes up the road, dashing their overall race hopes.

In 1996, Spaniard Miguel Indurain was on a quest for a record sixth Tour de France win. Jacques Anquetil, Eddy Merckx, and Bernard Hinault had all tried—and failed—before him. But Indurain was the first of the five-timers to win his Tours in straight succession. Nothing, it seemed, could keep him from number six.

After a week of flatland racing marked by wet and wicked weather, the 1996 Tour de France was already at the doorway to the Alps. On July 6, the pack launched onto the brutal climb to the finish at Les Arcs without a yellow jersey in its midst. Race leader Stéphane Heulot, of France, stung by a knee injury that left him crippled and in tears at the roadside, had been forced to abandon the stage. The Tour was in need of a new leader, and all eyes logically turned toward Miguel Indurain, the winner of the previous five editions of the race.

On the opening grades of the final climb, Indurain adopted his usual strong and stoic position on the bike. But this time, something seemed amiss. The Spaniard's face was drawn, and his eyes squinted with pain. Four miles from the summit finish, Luc Leblanc attacked. The Frenchman wasn't a threat for the overall win, and Indurain let him go, preferring to keep a stalking eye on his main rivals.

"Suddenly, I could feel the strength draining from my body," Indurain said later. "I drifted to the back of my group of riders. I understood that I was about to be in big trouble." The Spaniard had "bonked," entered that precipitous and violent pitch into exhaustion that all cyclists sooner or later encounter.

"I don't know how I survived to finish," a delirious Indurain said at Les Arcs on July 6, 1996.

His face contorted in pain, Indurain desperately demanded a water bottle with just under a mile to ride. Race regulations forbade food or drink in the finale of a stage. Indurain knew this, but he didn't care. In his deteriorating state, the choice between a drink of water and a 20-second penalty was simple.

"At the finish, I couldn't even see the road. I don't know how I made it to the line," Indurain, who had been so infallible the years before, admitted. Like Anquetil, Merckx, and Hinault before him, Indurain would see his career Tour de France tally stop at five.

CHAPTER 6

Team Players

Without them, there would be no Tour de France champions. The unsung teammates are the heroes in the shadows, responsible for the rise—or decline—of their team leader. Whether pacing him in the mountains or pushing him on the flats, they are the constant companions of a team's designated leader. Cycling, after all, is also a team sport.

6

A "Corpse" on the Podium

Maurice De Waele is sick, weakened to the point of no return. All he has left is courage—and a magnificent team.

Maurice De Waele's crusade is over: He wins the 1929 Tour in front of Italian Giuseppe Pancera *(center)* and his Belgian compatriot Jef Demuysere *(right)*.

In the Tour de France, a rider is often only as strong as his team. That mantra rung deafeningly true in 1929, when the Alcyon formation pushed, prodded, and literally carried illness-hit Belgian Maurice De Waele to the race's overall crown.

On the morning of the July 20, 1929, Tour stage between Grenoble and Evian, Alcyon team director Ludovic Feuillet was in a frenzy. It was an hour before the stage's start, and Feuillet's yellow-jersey-wearing team leader, Maurice De Waele, was nowhere to be seen. There was reason to fear the worst: For the previous few days, De Waele had been complaining of stomach pains and fever.

Word was that after enduring a sleepless night, the ill Belgian had fainted. So Feuillet had De Waele reanimated and ordered his teammates to escort him to the start line. "Surround him and help him, but do it with a smile," Feuillet instructed. "I don't want anyone to know how sick he is."

When the stage started, the term "bodyguard" took on a whole new dimension. In the hills, three Alcyon riders would push De Waele to the summits while the rest of the team controlled the pace in the peloton. Shoulder to shoulder, the Alcyon riders created a dam on the front line of the pack, forbidding all breakaway attempts. In the first 3 hours of the stage, the peloton covered only 30 miles.

The days passed, and the Alcyon team's tactics remained the same. Rival riders even complained that the Alcyon members would grab their saddles to extinguish even the slightest thoughts of breaking away.

When De Waele was confirmed as the race's winner in Paris, Tour de France director Henri Desgrange was incredulous, exclaiming, "How could a yellow jersey so easy to steal make it to Paris in first place? A cadaver has won the race!"

Racked by illness, De Waele won the Tour de France, thanks to his teammates.

On July 28, during the final stage between Dieppe and Paris, yellow jersey De Waele *(in front)* is sheltered by his teammate Julien Vervaecke *(in second position).*

6

René Vietto sheds tears after sacrificing his own race chances to help his team leader, Antonin Magne, on the stage between Ax-les-Thermes and Luchon on July 21, 1934.

The Altruist

René Vietto is furious. He screams, kicks, and cries. But he is also proud because he has done his job.

The annals of Tour de France history are filled with the names of the race's great champions—but rarely with the names of the teammates who helped put them on the podium. Sometimes, these yellow-jersey lieutenants sacrifice their own chances at reaching the Tour de France limelight. Case in point: René Vietto, who began the 1934 race as a simple "water boy" for Antonin Magne.

In his debut Tour de France, climbing ace René Vietto caused a sensation in the Alps, winning stages in Grenoble, Digne, and his hometown of Cannes. The public immediately branded Vietto as a potential race winner, but the Frenchman knew his place: At the 1934 Tour de France, his job was to assist his team leader, Antonin Magne.

And so Vietto did, on the stage between Perpignan and Ax-les-Thermes, when the yellow-jersey-wearing Magne crashed, destroying his front wheel. Vietto donated his bicycle to his team leader, allowing Magne to save his first place from the encroaching menace of Italian Guiseppe Martano. Vietto lost 5 agonizing minutes in the overall standings while awaiting a bike change.

The next day, the race raged toward Luchon. On the descent off the Portet d'Aspet, Vietto was setting the tempo at the front of the race and didn't see a technical mishap that left Magne with a broken chain. Martano, however, saw everything and seized his chance to accelerate the pace. Race leader Magne was at a loss. With no teammates within reach, the Frenchman knew that the overall lead was slipping away.

Suddenly, a disbelieving Magne saw a rider climbing back up the mountain. It was Vietto, who had been alerted by a race motorcycle of Magne's predicament. Once again, Vietto gave up his bicycle to his teammate. And once again, Vietto waited for a replacement, knowing full well that his chances for the stage win and a podium finish in Paris had been annihilated. The grateful race winner, Magne, singled out Vietto at the Tour's end in Paris, inviting the altruist to share his victory lap at the Parc des Princes velodrome.

Magne *(left)*, winner of the 1934 Tour, shares the race's spoils with Vietto, his teammate and savior.

6 Bartali Gets a Lifeline

Forget the race. Gino Bartali's life was saved by a teammate . . .

Gino Bartali *(with bike)* savors his victory in the stage from Aix-les-Bains to Grenoble on July 7, 1937, in the company of his teammate Francesco Camusso *(right)*. Neither one could have imagined what the next day would bring.

Rarely has beginner's luck been a factor at the Tour de France. Winning the world's toughest bike race requires experience. But in 1937, an Italian upstart named Gino Bartali appeared ready to rewrite the statistics.

Gino Bartali garnered great attention at the start of the 1937 Tour de France, the Italian's first attempt at the race. Just 22 years old, Bartali exuded a class and charisma that transcended the style of the rest of the riders in the race. Bartali hinted at his potential on the Tour's first climb, the Ballon d'Alsace. He then confirmed his star power in the Alps.

On the stage between Aix-les-Bains and Grenoble, Bartali made mincemeat of the tough mountain roads, winning the yellow jersey and relegating his rivals to a deficit of more than 9 minutes. He did this after starting the day 12 minutes behind in the overall standings. The Tour de France, it seemed, was already signed, sealed, and delivered in the name of Bartali.

The next day, July 8, the race through the Alps continued on rain-slicked roads. In a small group off the front, Bartali was glued to the wheel of his teammate Jules Rossi. At the exit of the town of Embrun, Rossi slipped on a small wooden bridge over a mountain stream that was raging because of the stormy weather. Bartali couldn't avoid his fallen teammate and pitched over the guardrail into the torrents below.

Bartali's teammate Francesco Camusso saved Bartali from certain drowning, but on the banks of the river, the diagnosis was grave: Bartali had suffered a painful blow to the chest, and his left arm and knee were covered in blood. He was in bad shape. The Italian somehow finished the stage, but he lost 10 minutes in the general classification. In the following days, Bartali's condition deteriorated, as his river swim reawakened a dormant case of bronchitis. His hopes of regaining the yellow jersey came to an end when he abandoned the race in Marseille.

At the start of the 1938 Tour de France, race revelation Bartali was determined to avoid the bad luck that haunted him the year before.

6

His persistence made Vietto a favorite of the French fans.

Vietto's Last Stand

The Tour tests character as much as endurance, which made Rene the "King."

At the start of the 1947 Tour de France, René "King René" Vietto was the favorite of the French fans. Still fresh in their collective memory was Vietto's altruism in the 1934 race, when the French rider sacrificed his own chances for those of his team leader, Antonin Magne. Finally, it seemed, Vietto was about to get his revenge.

As early as the second stage of the 1947 race, René Vietto went on the attack; he grabbed the yellow jersey after a heroic and solitary escape between Lille and Brussels. True, Vietto lost the race lead soon thereafter, but the fans' unconditional love for this veteran of the pre-World-War era gave Vietto wings. He was back in the yellow jersey by the ninth stage of the Tour.

The battles for the yellow jersey were merciless: Vietto versus Edouard Fachleitner, Pierre Brambilla, and particularly his fellow Frenchman Jean Robic. "This is a cakewalk...I'm invincible," Robic regularly whispered to Vietto in psych-out tactics.

King René, however, was infallible. The Frenchman was still in yellow on July 18, the 19th stage of the Tour de France. A daunting 86-mile time trial between Vannes and Saint-Brieuc awaited the riders, and the day would prove to be fatal for Vietto's overall hopes.

Vietto crumbled, finishing 15th on the stage and losing the yellow jersey. Devastated, he hinted at quitting the race. "A champion of your caliber can't quit like that," implored Georges Briquet, director of the French national team.

"What? A Vietto doesn't quit! He bows out gracefully!" replied the Frenchman.

Vietto nonetheless continued the 1947 Tour de France and finished in fifth place overall. Many, however, tried to explain his fall from grace two days before the finish. A rumor circulated that on that hot July 18 day, Vietto may have refreshed himself—and sabotaged his chances—by mixing beer, cider, and perhaps something of a stronger proof while riding.

Vietto often led the Tour but never won.

6

The Perfect Domestique

He is ashamed. He considers himself a traitor. He stole the star power of his team leader . . .

Gino Bartali, Andrea Carrea, Alfredo Binda, and Fausto Coppi *(left to right).* On July 4, 1952, at the start of the stage between Lausanne and Alpe d'Huez, the yellow jersey was on unexpected shoulders.

Toiling in the shadows for the glory of the team leader—that's the job of the majority of the pack, the "domestiques" of the race. But sometimes, doing one's job—and the luck of the draw—can offer a simple soldier his 15 minutes of Tour de France fame.

Andrea "Sandrino" Carrea was worried. On the ninth stage of the 1952 Tour de France, the most devoted teammate of Italian great Fausto Coppi had a sneaking suspicion that the pack was preparing an onslaught of attacks. When Carrea informed Coppi of his sixth sense, Coppi gently brushed him off: "Keep an eye on whomever you'd like, Sandrino."

And so when 10 riders bubbled off the front with 87 miles still to ride, Carrea went, too. The escape ended up trumping the pack, and as Carrea ambled to his team's hotel, he wondered if the peloton would make the finish in enough time to save the yellow jersey of Italian Fiorenzo Magni.

Several minutes later, two police officers knocked on Carrea's door. The Italian's confusion turned to shock when he learned the motive of their visit: Carrea was wanted on the race's podium. Because of the time split registered by the break, he was the new yellow jersey of the race!

Instead of joy, Carrea was filled with terror; he felt as if he had betrayed his team. As Carrea slipped on the yellow jersey, he shed tears of shame.

"What are you crying for?" Coppi asked after the yellow-jersey ceremony.

"I don't have the right to wear it, Fausto. Not a simple domestique like me," Carrea said.

Touched, Coppi vowed to help Carrea keep the yellow jersey for a few more days. Unfortunately, the race dictated otherwise. On the very next stage, French contender Jean Robic launched a brutal attack that required Coppi's attention. The Italian won the stage at the summit of Alpe d'Huez and usurped the overall race lead—to the delight of Carrea.

"Ah, that's much better! Carrea said. "It wasn't right that a soldier be in front of his captain."

Throughout the race, Coppi *(in front)* had to fend off the attacks of his future runner-up, Stan Ockers *(in second position)*, and Frenchman Jean Robic, who finished fifth overall in Paris.

6

White Lies

A champion amounts to nothing without his teammates—or for that matter, his team director.

July 18, 1955: Marcel Bidot encourages Louison Bobet during the Frenchman's solo escape on Mont Ventoux.

In difficult times, Tour de France team directors must be more than master tacticians. They also have to be cheerleaders to cajole impossible efforts from their riders. And if a little white lie needs to be told—well, so be it.

On July 18, 1955, the Tour de France had a date with Mont Ventoux. The Giant of Provence, the mountain is a barren, hulking ascent with not an inch of shade on its lunarlike summit. In 1955, a heat wave baked the race, and several favorites, notably Ferdi Kubler and Jean Malléjac, had already cracked off the back.

French rider Louison Bobet, however, got the Ventoux's goat, escaping solo and cresting the summit with a healthy margin on climbing ace Charly Gaul, of Luxembourg.

Thirty-seven miles still remained before the finish in Avignon, and Bobet, tiring by the minute, was far from home free. The Frenchman made a hand sign, drawing his team car alongside him. "If my lead drops below 1 minute, let me know and I'll cut my effort," Bobet said to his team director, Marcel Bidot.

Bidot gave his rider the thumbs-up, but the director had a different plan brewing. Bidot knew that Bobet's confidence had wavered throughout the race. The two-time defending champion had become the primary target of the rival teams, and the pressure was beginning to weigh on Bobet. To boost Bobet's spirits, Bidot was dead set on encouraging his rider to the stage victory—at all costs.

When Bobet's lead dipped below the 1-minute mark, Bidot only cheered his rider on with more gusto. And on each ensuing straightaway section, Bidot strategically placed his car directly behind Bobet so that the Frenchman wouldn't be able to see the three riders launched in pursuit of him. Unaware of his precarious position, Bobet fought to the finish, winning the stage and restoring the morale he needed to win his third consecutive Tour de France.

July 25 in Saint-Gaudens: Bidot *(right)* looks on as Charly Gaul *(second from left)* wins his second stage of the 1955 Tour de France and Bobet *(center)* takes over the yellow jersey.

6

Internal Conflict

He thought he was the outcast, the black sheep of his team. And then he found a friend. Then two, and then, lo and behold, the support of the whole squad.

On July 4, 1967, on the ascent of the Thuin climb, Roger Pingeon escaped with incredible ease. He won the stage in Jambes by 6 minutes and usurped the yellow jersey.

Frenchman Roger Pingeon had a temper. He was often in conflict with his teammates, his team directors, or the race organizers. Because of his prickly personality, Pingeon was rarely given the support his talent might have deserved.

On July 4, 1967, the Tour de France butted up against the Wall of Thuin, a mean-spirited climb of stubborn cobblestones. In many ways, the hill mirrored Roger Pingeon's character. The former plumber had lost the first years of his cycling career to the war in Algeria. When he did return to the peloton, Pingeon could be a loose cannon. Capricious, he once abandoned a race because his team director couldn't get him a wheel change as quickly as Pingeon would have liked. The Frenchman's reputation took a hard hit, as did his morale.

But on stage five of the 1967 Tour de France, between Roubaix, France, and Jambes, Belgium, Pingeon suddenly got a helping hand. His teammate, the always jovial Jean Stablinski, encouraged Pingeon to bridge up to a breakaway of 12 riders. Pingeon took the advice, and on the Wall of Thuin climb, the Frenchman dropped the rest of the break with surprising ease.

At the top of the hill, Pingeon tucked in for a ballistic solo race to the finish. The Frenchman at first had just the stage win to savor. But 6 minutes later—the time it took for the rest of the race to catch up to Pingeon—he also usurped the yellow jersey. Later in the race, French idol Raymond Poulidor offered his services to his teammate Pingeon, helping the outcast of the peloton all the way to the overall race win.

Raymond Poulidor *(left)* congratulates his teammate Pingeon, winner of the 1967 Tour de France.

6

Merckx Fights a Friend

The Cannibal felt betrayed. Worse, the slight came from his best teammate and friend.

On July 15, 1969, Eddy Merckx *(left)* attacks his own teammate, Martin Van Den Bossche, on the ascent of the Tourmalet.

Even for a champion of the ilk of Eddy Merckx, the Tour de France isn't just the cold reality of seconds won and lost, attacks, and calculated strategies. It's also a story of friendship between teammates—for better or for worse.

"Take it easy. There's still the Aubisque climb to come," team director Guillaume Driessens cautioned his star rider, Eddy Merckx. It was July 15, 1969, and Merckx had just attacked on the ascent of the Tourmalet, dropping not only his biggest rivals—Roger Pingeon, Raymond Poulidor, and André Zimmerman—but also his own teammate, Martin Van Den Bossche, who had been hovering solo off the front.

Alone at the Tourmalet's summit, Merckx refused to relent. The Belgian tightened up his toe straps and continued his madcap effort. But why? Felice Gimondi, second in the overall standings, was already 9 minutes and 29 seconds behind the Cannibal. Barring disaster, the Tour was already decided.

Merckx, however, appeared willing to bring disaster upon himself. Fighting solo on the Aubisque climb—and with an 8-minute advantage on the rest of the race—Merckx suddenly hit a wall with 9 miles still to ride. "I'm dead," he confided to team director Driessens.

"The others are even deader than you!" Driessens replied to boost his rider's morale.

Merckx survived to the finish. He then acquiesced when questioned by the press about the insanity of his escape. "I attacked on the Tourmalet because I felt betrayed," he said. "Martin Van Den Bossche, my teammate, wanted to reach the Tourmalet first."

At this point, confusion reigned. Was the Cannibal delirious? Van Den Bossche wasn't just Merckx's teammate, he was also one of the Belgian's best friends and his roommate on the Tour de France.

"Bossche told me the other day that he was leaving the team at the end of the season, that he'd already signed a contract to ride for someone else," Merckx explained. "I was disappointed, almost angry. So I attacked to be the first to the top of the Tourmalet."

Merckx *(left)* with his team director, Guillaume Driessens

6

Zoetemelk: Finally!

Nothing, it seems, can stand in Joop Zoetemelk's way. His team is the strongest, wielding an ironclad fist over the Tour de France.

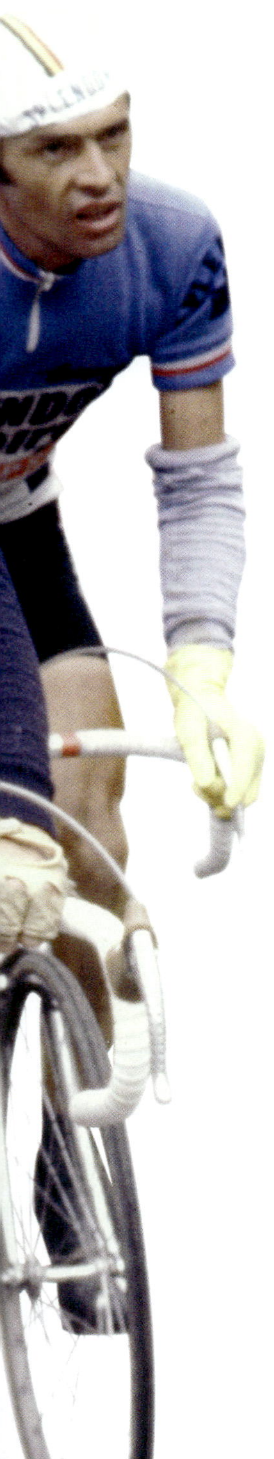

In 1980, Joop Zoetemelk was desperately seeking his first Tour de France win. The Dutchman had finished second five times at the world's greatest bike race. The 1980 Tour would be his 10th—and likely his last chance for overall victory.

The race in 1980 began just like its two previous editions: under the heavy hand of defending champion Bernard Hinault. The Frenchman dominated the early stages to stake his claim on the yellow jersey. But in Pau on July 9, Hinault announced that he was abandoning the race. Crippled by tendonitis in a knee, the Badger could badger no more. Joop Zoetemelk, second in the overall standings, inherited the yellow jersey—and the role of overall race favorite.

Because he had finished second so many times, Zoetemelk ordered his powerful Raleigh team to ride a controlled race. The Dutchman didn't want to take any unnecessary risks. The race, however, chose otherwise. Two miles from the summit of the Pra-Loup climb, Zoetemelk crashed, deeply cutting an elbow and thigh. Panicked to see his Tour dream disappearing before his eyes, Zoetemelk gritted through the pain, finished the stage, and saved his overall lead. But for how long?

The next day's stage was another rude mountain test, and a still-aching Zoetemelk found himself floundering 2 minutes off the back on the first climb. But the Dutchman's team rallied to his assistance, pacing Zoetemelk to summit after summit. Inspired by his team's show of confidence, Zoetemelk breathed a second wind. The race's eternal runner-up recovered his deficit on the gruesome grades of the Madeleine climb and flew on to his first and only Tour de France triumph.

On July 10, 1980, the door to the Tour de France overall win opened wide for Joop Zoetemelk *(left)* after Bernard Hinault abandoned the race. Here, Zoetemelk rides alongside Dutchman Hennie Kuiper *(second from left)* and Swede Sven-Ake Nilsson *(right front).*

Zoetemelk tries on the yellow jersey in Luchon. He kept it to the race's end in Paris.

6

Double Trouble

They are two, but between them they appear to have the strength of 10. Greg LeMond and Bernard Hinault, united by the bonds of their team.

In 1986, Bernard Hinault was on the cusp of a record sixth win at the Tour de France. But one year earlier, the Frenchman had given his word to help his American teammate Greg LeMond to his first Tour title. With history on the line, would Hinault keep his promise?

In 1985, Greg LeMond rode second fiddle to assist in the record-tying fifth Tour de France win of his teammate Bernard Hinault. A gentlemen's agreement between the two cyclists stipulated that Hinault would return the favor the following year. But from the start of the 1986 Tour de France, a not-so-friendly rivalry developed between LeMond and Hinault. With the prospect of a record sixth Tour win tantalizingly within reach, Hinault's message was clear: May the best man win.

In the early stages of the race, both the American and the Frenchman won their battles, but on July 21, at the foot of Alpe d'Huez, it was LeMond who appeared ready to win the war. The American was in the yellow jersey, and Hinault was in third place. Sandwiched between the two La Vie Claire teammates, in second, was the dangerous Swiss rider Urs Zimmermann. To ensure that the yellow jersey remained a team affair, Hinault and LeMond had to attack on the stage to Alpe d'Huez. Hinault launched the hostilities on the Galibier climb. Quickly joined by LeMond, the two men raced 56 miles off the front before butting up against the mythic switchbacks of Alpe d'Huez.

"Grab my wheel and stick close. That way nothing can happen," Hinault told LeMond. The Frenchman's advice was given in part to protect the American from the manic throngs of fans lining the roadside. The French public, wishing for a record sixth Hinault win, shot the occasional epithet and unsavory gesture at LeMond.

Together, the two men climbed. But at the summit of Alpe d'Huez, neither one of them broke into a sprint. Instead, Hinault and LeMond joined hands and crossed the finish in unison. The best men had won.

Bernard Hinault *(right)* leading his teammate Greg LeMond on the Alpe d'Huez climb on July 21, 1986

The day after their one-two punch on Alpe d'Huez, LeMond *(left)* and Hinault kick back during a rest day.

6

Crash Course

Armstrong's luck runs out, but his will overcomes.

In bicycle racing, being a team player doesn't just mean supporting one's own team. It also means respecting riders on competing teams, knowing when to launch an attack and when to hold back—even if it might hurt your position in the race. German Jan Ullrich knows these rules of sportsmanship all too well, as he demonstrated—to his own disadvantage—at the 2003 Tour de France.

A crash nearly changed the face of the 2003 Tour. On the race's 15th stage, on the climb to the finish at Luz Ardiden in the Pyrenees, Lance Armstrong was suddenly whipped to the ground. Slow-motion television replays showed that the American, hugging a right-hand road barrier formed by a wall of fans, clipped a souvenir bag held by a young spectator.

The instant worldwide reaction was stupefaction, but then a very pertinent question began to be asked: What would Jan Ullrich do? Chances are the German asked himself the very same question. After avoiding the crash by the skin of his teeth, Ullrich was suddenly faced with a dilemma. Ahead lay a wide-open, Armstrong-free road. The German could have accelerated away, and in doing so, he likely would have won the Tour de France.

Ullrich, however, chose a different fork in the road. Adhering to the unwritten Tour de France rule that you never attack a yellow jersey when he's down, the German cut his effort and waited for Armstrong to ride back into the race. It was the just thing to do; the American had shown the same courtesy to Ullrich two years prior when the German rode off course and crashed.

Ullrich's altruism was admirable, but it did cost him the overall race. As soon as Armstrong rejoined the leaders of the pack, the American, his veins coursing with adrenaline and anger, attacked. The U.S. Postal rider dropped all, soloing free for the stage win and putting a definitive lock on his fifth straight Tour victory.

Shortly after attacking, Armstrong and Mayo are pulled down (by accident).

Ullrich waits for Armstrong, proving his professionalism.

6

Victory Delivered by U.S. Postal

When he needed them most, Armstrong's team pulls through.

On July 9, the U.S. Postal team was intent on stamping its dominance on stage four's team time trial, a discipline the squad had never before won at the Tour de France.

Despite a sharp wind and a slow start, the American team ratcheted into gear. By midrace, U.S. Postal was flying. And at the finish, they had sealed first on the stage, distancing Joseba Beloki's ONCE formation by 30 seconds and Jan Ullrich's Bianchi squad by 43 seconds. The yellow jersey went to Armstrong's loyal Colombian lieutenant, Victor Hugo Peña. It was a Tour de France first for the South American nation.

After the team time trial, U.S. Postal seemed to have a vise grip on the Tour de France. But for the first time in five years,

All nine riders of U.S. Postal were in top form in 2003.

cracks began to show in Armstrong's armor. Challenged in the mountains, Armstrong struggled in the yellow jersey. And on the race's 12th stage, Ullrich dropped the American by 1 minute and 30 seconds.

Tested by his own shortcomings, crashes, and the hypermotivated Ullrich, Armstrong had never been closer to losing the Tour de France. But thanks to the solidarity of his U.S. Postal team, the American was paced back into the yellow-jersey hunt.

On the race's decisive day, a time trial to Nantes in northwestern France, Lady Luck smiled on Armstrong. Ullrich crashed on a rain-slicked corner, securing Armstrong his fifth straight win—1 minute ahead of the hapless German.

For the 2003 edition of the Tour de France, Lance Armstrong had a double dose of motivation: The 2003 race represented a possible record-equaling fifth straight win for the American, and it was also the centenary edition of the world's greatest bike race. Armstrong did reach his goal, but he didn't do it on his own. In 2003, more than in any other year, the Texan owed a big thank you to his team.

Pena becomes the first Postal rider, other than Armstrong, to wear yellow.

July 6, 1960: Roger Rivière on the wheel of yellow jersey Gastone Nencini between Pau and Luchon

Rivière's Tragic Tale

The history of the Tour de France is not just fun, games, and glory. Sometimes tragedy gets in the way.

On July 10, 1960, Roger Rivière crashed on the descent off the Perjuret climb. Pitched 50 feet into a ravine, the badly hurt Frenchman, just 24 years old, tucked into a fetal position. Help was on its way, directed by fellow French rider Louis Rostollan, who had fortunately seen where Rivière had fallen.

A helicopter hovered over Rivière, but evacuation to the hospital was delayed by a local landowner. Fearing for his crops, the farmer had brandished a shotgun, temporarily preventing the helicopter from landing.

As Rivière awaited rescue, he thought of the current stage between Millau and Avignon. Thanks to a breakaway earlier in the race, Rivière and the Italian Nencini had a 14-minute advance on the rest of the pack. At the top of the Perjuret, Nencini—a master descender—had begun the downhill with Rivière glued to his wheel. The Frenchman was determined to match wits with Nencini—until that fateful corner and a too-hard grab of the brakes.

At first, the medical word was of a miracle: Rivière should within weeks be back in action. But at the end of August, French cycling legend Raphaël Geminiani visited Rivière in rehabilitation.

"Raphaël, go find out what's happening," a distraught Rivière said. "They're telling me my cycling days are done."

After crashing on the descent off the Perjuret on July 10, Rivière is transferred by helicopter to the hospital in Montpellier.

In 1960, Roger Rivière wanted to play his own Tour de France hand. Dissatisfied with his role of support rider, the Frenchman disobeyed his team's direction and joined a breakaway effort that lofted him into the hunt for the yellow jersey. The race leadership, however, still belonged to Italian Gastone Nencini, the best downhiller in the bunch.

Geminiani consulted Rivière's surgeon, who revealed that an undetected fractured vertebra had since solidified and damaged nerves beyond repair. Rivière would never ride again.

Rivière and his wife during a rest day in Millau, the day before his crash

7

The End of the Road

Tragedy—and controversy—strike the Tour.

Simpson's effort on Mount Ventoux would be his last.

On July 13, 1967, Tom Simpson rode to the red line of his physical reserves. The British former world champion was free-falling in the Tour de France's overall standings; he sat 8 minutes and 20 seconds behind the yellow jersey, Frenchman Roger Pingeon. Simpson's goal, however, was to make the Tour's podium. To do so, he knew that the climb to the summit of Mont Ventoux would be do-or-die.

At the stage's midpoint, temperatures were already spiking into the 90s. Tom Simpson stalked at the back of the peloton, which was policed by the French team for overall leader Pingeon and sentimental favorite Raymond Poulidor.

Pacing with the leaders, Simpson attacked 3 miles before the summit of the Ventoux. It is a behemoth of a climb made all the more suffocating by the peak's lunar landscape, barren of trees and therefore scorched by the burning sun.

Simpson's solo move failed. The Briton weaved from roadside to roadside, sapped of his strength. He soldiered on, but a mile of climbing later, Simpson tumbled. "Put me back on my bike," he implored. Those would be his last words. Simpson rode a hundred more feet before falling again and losing consciousness. A spectator administered mouth-to-mouth resuscitation as an emergency helicopter arrived on the scene.

But it was too late. At 5:40 p.m. on July 13, 1967, Simpson was pronounced dead. Witnesses would later confide that they had seen Simpson drink two glasses of alcohol before attacking the Ventoux climb. Amphetamines were also found in the jersey pocket of the deceased cyclist.

The next day, the peloton allowed Simpson's teammate Barry Hoban to win a stage in the memory of Simpson. It was a bitter win for the British team members, who could do nothing to bring back their leader. Heat, alcohol, drugs, and Mont Ventoux: a dangerous—and deadly—cocktail.

Despite efforts by officials and spectators, Simpson would not survive.

7

Pushed Around

Fan support can get a little fanatical at the Tour de France.

Raymond Riotte doing the best that he can in the mountains.

Fans are dissuaded from running next to the riders of the Tour de France. And giving the competitors a helping push in the mountains is strictly prohibited by race regulations. Fans clogging up the road can only lead to trouble. But in the free-thinking liberation of the 1968 Tour de France, everyone did as he or she pleased.

In France and the world over, 1968 was a time of revolution. Liberalism and hippie ideals were à la mode. The Tour de France, too, was swept up in the winds of change. French rider Lucien Aimar defected from the national team, claiming, "We all wave our own flags. The black of anarchy suits me just fine!"

The first week of the race was a monotone procession of flat stages dominated by the race's sprinters. Tour de France organizers chastised the press for focusing too much on the lull that had hit the race. Members of the media, themselves embracing the new ideals of liberalism, went on strike, strewing their notebooks and recorders in the middle of the race route outside Bordeaux.

Finally, the Tour de France found some semblance of order in the mountains. The race quickly picked up its pace—too quickly for Raymond Riotte's comfort. The Frenchman dropped backward on the first climb and found himself struggling at the back of the bunch. Suddenly, a spectator jumped from the crowd and began to push Riotte. It was a pleasing sensation for the Frenchman, who decided to prolong the push as long as possible. Riotte promised the Good Samaritan that he would send an autographed photo after the race, but to do that, he would need the fan's name and address. Huffing and puffing, the thrilled spectator spelled out his name and street coordinates. And by the time the fan had finished pushing Riotte, the refreshed rider had traveled a good 100 yards without a single pedal stroke.

The fan never got Riotte's photo.

Riotte's career was marked by a solitary day in the yellow jersey: July 6, 1967, after the stage between Metz and Strasbourg.

7

Thévenet: Out of Sorts

All was forgotten: the effort, the pain, the stage finish still far up the road. That's amnesia.

It's unlikely that Bernard Thévenet will ever forget the July 9 stage of the 1972 Tour de France. Ironically, during the stage itself, the Frenchman, the victim of a horrific crash, could barely remember his own name.

Thévenet's mind was foggy. The bike he was riding seemed odd. It wasn't the same one he had earlier, was it? And there must have been a storm, because the road was wet. The Frenchman looked at his team director, Gaston Plaud, and asked, "Where are we? Where are we going?"

A distressed Plaud couldn't respond.

"Gaston, this is the Tour de France, right?" Thévenet asked.

A trail of blood ran down Thévenet's face. The Frenchman understood that he must have crashed. He began to piece together facts that still made sense. As of the night before, he had been well placed in the overall Tour de France standings, sitting in sixth, 1 minute and 30 seconds behind Frenchman Cyril Guimard.

Then he recalled the climb to the top of the Soulor in the company of Belgian Lucien Van Impe. The duo had been chasing Eddy Merckx. Later, on a downhill, there was a crash. Spaniard Luis Ocana had fallen in front of Thévenet. This the Frenchman was sure of, because in his mind he saw Ocana's spectacular flip over his handlebars. After that, however, it all went black. Later, Thévenet was told that his fellow Frenchman Alain Santy had also crashed. Less lucky, Santy was out of the race with multiple fractures.

Thévenet's team director advised his rider to wait for the arrival of his teammate Wilfried David. David, immediately aware that Thévenet was barely coherent, paced the Frenchman back into the race. Slowly but surely, Thévenet's wits returned, and at the end of the stage, he was lucid enough to detail his predicament to the press.

After a night in observation at the hospital, Thévenet returned to the race. The Frenchman made it home to Paris in ninth position overall, 37 minutes behind the winner, Merckx.

On July 9, 1972, Bernard Thévenet crashed on the descent off the Soulor climb. It would take him several hours to start thinking straight.

In the Tour's final week, Thévenet was back with the race's best. Here, he is in the company of José Manuel Fuente, Eddy Merckx, Régis Ovion, and Joop Zoetemelk *(left to right).*

The Tour on Strike

Chaotic stage starts, impossible timetables. The peloton finally decided that enough was enough.

July 12, 1978: The peloton stops in protest just several hundred feet from the finish at Valence d'Agen. Michel Pollentier *(polka-dot jersey)*, Bernard Hinault *(center)*, and Freddy Maertens *(right)* represent the movement.

As in any job, being a professional cyclist is not all fun and games. The peloton's riders were disgruntled with their working conditions during the 1978 edition of the race. On July 12, they decided to do something about it.

The stage start in Tarbes was at 7:30 a.m.–ludicrously early for a peloton racked with fatigue after a stretch of racing in the Pyrenees. With more climbing on the horizon and an exhausting procession of late-night hotel arrivals and stage starts scheduled at dawn, the riders needed a break.

At the beginning of the Tarbes stage, the pace was slow. Any breakaway attempts were squelched, and the offending riders were reminded that the race needed to rest. Riders exchanged glances and discussed strategy among themselves. A decision was made: They would not participate in the upcoming bonus sprint.

No one in the pack forced the tempo, and the race lollygagged at a snail's pace that would have the riders at the finish too late for the next stage–a short race scheduled for the same afternoon! Furious, the Tour directors assembled the various team directors, but there was nothing to be done. "It's out of our hands," the teams lamented.

The race rolled into the stage-finish town of Valence d'Agen 2 hours slower than expected. Suddenly, a rumor circulated in the pack that organizers were planning to cancel all of the stage's cash rewards. That was the final straw. Less than a mile from the finish, the peloton put its foot down–literally. The race came to a screeching halt, and the riders walked the remaining distance to the finish.

The stage was officially cancelled by race organizers, who donated the day's prize money to the social-work offices of the city of Valence d'Agen. Race favorite and strike figurehead Bernard Hinault was booed by some of the fans. Others, however, were more philosophical: "At least we get to see them longer when they're on foot!"

Jacques Goddet tries to convince the exhausted riders to pick up the Tour de France fight. Here he rides alongside André Chalmel, one of the leaders of the pack's resistance.

June 30, 1985: Eric Vanderaerden *(yellow jersey)* is beaten in the sprint by Rudy Matthijs *(in front)* and Sean Kelly to finish third on the stage to Vitré.

7

The Invisible Man

Eric Vanderaerden had no business winning this time trial. That's what everybody, including Vanderaerden, thought.

When Eric Vanderaerden launched into his individual time trial in Villard-de-Lans on July 11, 1985, the last thing on the Belgian's mind was achieving victory in the stage. On the previous day's road stage, Vanderaerden had finished in 142nd place, nearly 25 minutes off the pace.

Who will win a Tour de France time trial is generally a daylong mystery. The riders roll out in reverse order of the general classification, meaning the top contenders always go last.

On July 11, Eric Vanderaerden was one of the first competitors to encounter the day's 20-mile race against the clock in Villard-de-Lans. The Belgian sprinter didn't expect great things for the time trial. He had already enjoyed a successful Tour de France. The second-place finisher in the prologue, Vanderaerden had worn the yellow jersey for three days before giving up an eternity of time in the mountains.

On the Villard-de-Lans time trial, Vanderaerden stopped the clock at a respectable 41 minutes. Not a stellar time, but one that allowed the Belgian to take the early lead and to hope for a top-15 finish on the stage. Satisfied with his effort, Vanderaerden returned to his team's hotel to shower. At the finish, no one had congratulated the Belgian. The press hadn't thought to interview him. The real race for the stage would play out between the favorites later in the afternoon.

Phil Anderson *(left)* and Vanderaerden *(yellow jersey)* side by side between Lorient and Vitré

Suddenly, a stiff headwind began to blow across the time-trial course. One by one, the remaining riders tried—but failed—to beat Vanderaerden's time. The last starters were now filing to the start house. One of them, surely, would beat the Belgian.

But the intermediate time splits didn't lie: Vanderaerden was poised for the stage win. Rushed back to the finish line by motorcycle, the Belgian witnessed race favorite Bernard Hinault complete his turn on the time-trial course—more than a minute slower than did Vanderaerden, now officially the stage's winner.

A career-long team rider, Massimo Ghirotto was the surprise winner of the stage.

7

Wrong Way Bouvatier

The road to glory is full of obstacles. Just ask Philippe Bouvatier . . .

Forget the overall race win. Most Tour de France riders dream of winning just one stage. In 1988, Frenchman Philippe Bouvatier was so close—and yet so far—from making his stage-winning dreams come true.

Philippe Bouvatier had been pegged as a potential star of French cycling. Impressive as an amateur—some even compared the Frenchman to the great Jacques Anquetil—Bouvatier was nevertheless having trouble integrating into the professional ranks. In four years as a pro cyclist, he had yet to notch a single racing success. At the start of the 1988 Tour de France, the 24-year-old decided it was time he made a name for himself.

On the July 17 tough mountain stage between Blagnac and Guzet-Neige, Bouvatier saw his window of opportunity. The Frenchman wasn't a risk to the overall leaders, who were comfortably riding race control around Pedro Delgado. The Spaniard was virtually guaranteed the Tour de France win.

Bouvatier launched a breakaway effort. At the halfway point of the final climb, just three men were left off the front: Bouvatier, Scotsman Robert Millar, and Italian Massimo Ghirotto. Bouvatier accelerated mercilessly on the climb. In the final mile, the Frenchman found himself alone, racing toward a certain stage win.

With 300 yards to ride, the team cars in front of Bouvatier began to honk frantically. The gendarmes watching the route gesticulated wildly, but Bouvatier saw none of it. Head down and fighting for the line, the Frenchman had taken a wrong turn with the finish line nearly in sight. Ghirotto didn't make the same mistake, and he stole the stage from Bouvatier. His mistake realized, the Frenchman did an about-face, but he trailed to the finish 13 seconds too late.

Disbelief filled the face of Philippe Bouvatier, who finished second on the stage to Guzet-Neige on July 17, 1988.

Bouvatier finds the finish in Guzet-Neige 13 seconds behind Ghirotto.

7

Tony's Bad Luck

The strongest man doesn't always win the Tour de France, because once the bad luck begins . . .

Tony Rominger *(polka-dot jersey)* and Miguel Indurain racing between Andorra and St. Lary-Soulon July 21, 1993

At the start of the 1993 Tour de France, two-time defending champion Miguel Indurain wisely pointed out Tony Rominger as his principal rival. The 32-year-old Swiss rider was in flying form. And if it hadn't been for a wicked string of bad luck, Rominger could have won the whole Tour de France shebang.

"Tony Rominger? He's the biggest question mark I have in this race. I think he's very strong," said Indurain, of Spain, before the 1993 Tour. The reigning champion's prediction was spot-on; for the entirety of the three-week race, Rominger would be a constant thorn in Indurain's side.

And if a procession of bizarre mishaps would not have occurred, Rominger might have deposed King Indurain from his Tour de France throne. Unfortunately, luck was not with the Swiss contender. First, two of Rominger's Team Clas riders abandoned the race before the crucial team time trial. Reduced to seven riders—and then losing one more during the stage—the Clas formation lost 3 minutes in the stage before being hit with an additional 1-minute penalty for pushing a flagging rider back into the team's rhythm.

Then, on the individual race against the clock at Madine Lake, a flash storm decided to unleash its fury exactly when Rominger was about to take his turn on the course. "From 33 miles per hour, my speedometer suddenly crashed to less than 24!" the Swiss lamented at the end of the stage before noting that he had suffered a puncture in the final mile and limped to the finish on a flat rear tire.

"I can't believe this is happening," Rominger said. "It's entirely unfair." The Swiss enjoyed a brief reversal of fortune in the Alps, brilliantly winning two stages. Bad luck, however, returned in the Pyrenees. Misinformed on the topography of a stage finish at altitude, Rominger flubbed his gear selection and missed out on what would have otherwise been an easy stage triumph.

Rominger won the July 27 time trial between Brétigny-sur-Orge and Montlhéry, a show of force that earned him second overall at the 1993 Tour de France.

7

An Unclassy Act

Sprinters will risk everything for a win, even the win itself...

Erik Zabel has won more green jerseys than anyone but was caught cheating here.

July 11, 1997—it was the sixth stage of the Tour de France, 136 miles between Le Blanc and Marennes. The peloton was in a nervous tizzy from the start of the stage. And by its end, the racers had definitively lost their wits.

With the mountains looming on the horizon, the Tour de France's sprinters were eager for a final shot at glory. The pack was fraught with tension, an emotion amplified by a series of mass crashes throughout the stage. At the day's end, Erik Zabel, of Germany, was disqualified from the stage for head-butting a rival in the final straightaway. Djamolidine Abdoujaparov, of Uzbekistan, was disqualified from the entire race because the sprint master had tested positive for a banned substance.

Belgian champion Tom Steels also got in on the stage's shenanigans. The Mapei rider was bothered by Frédéric Moncassin, a Frenchman with a reputation for having an overly aggressive sprint style.

In the final sprint, Steels and Moncassin jostled elbow to elbow. Who started the hostilities will never be known, but the slow-motion television replay didn't lie: It showed Steels sitting up and flinging a water bottle at Moncassin at the apex of the sprint.

Steels let loose his emotions, and his water bottle.

The Belgian said Moncassin had tried to punch him out of the way, but the race's judges put the full responsibility for the incident on Steels. The Belgian was first disqualified on the stage and then booted from the race altogether for "violent behavior toward another competitor."

"I was very angry," Steels explained. "In the heat of the moment, you sometimes do things you might regret."

7

Zülle: The Crash Man

The Passage du Gois suddenly had a worldwide reputation, much to the chagrin of Alex Zülle.

On July 5, 1999, the Passage du Gois, which links the island of Noirmoutier to mainland France, was the stage for a spectacular mass crash.

Alex Zülle never won the Tour de France, a sad fact the Swiss rider would partially attribute to his incredibly bad racing luck. Zülle had an impressive knack for crashing right when the race stakes were at their highest.

On July 5, 1999, the Tour de France traversed the Passage du Gois, a short stretch of road that links the Island of Noirmoutier to mainland France and rises above sea level only at low tide. As the race approached the 2.5-mile-long passage, nerves in the pack were running high. A blustery crosswind swept the race, and a fine layer of sea salt had turned the road surface slick.

Alex Zülle, celebrating his 31st birthday, began the crossing of the Passage du Gois with trepidation. The Swiss rider already had 19 screws in his shoulder, the result of a crash two years earlier. Suddenly, just in front of Zülle, a rider slipped and crashed. With nowhere to go on the sliver-thin Passage du Gois, the race was brought to a chaotic halt. Zülle rode off the road, crashing shoulder-first into a spectator, who helped him back to his feet. "I was back up and I was ready to ride, but I was blocked—trapped in the middle of the Atlantic Ocean!" Zülle said later.

The crash had cut the peloton in two. A small pack of 20 riders—those lucky enough to be in front of the crash—accelerated away. In that front group were most of the overall race favorites, and their new goal for the day was to eliminate Zülle from yellow-jersey contention.

After finally becoming untangled and navigating the Passage du Gois, Zülle's Banesto team members did their best to pull their leader back into the race. Their efforts, however, were in vain. Zülle finished the stage 6 minutes behind its winner, Tom Steels, of Belgium. José Miguel Echavarri, the Banesto team director, made no bones about what had happened: "No one won the Tour de France today," he said. "Alex, however, lost it."

Just minutes after the crash on the Passage du Gois, Alex Zülle, here in front of Ivan Gotti, tries in vain to make up for lost time.

7

Shock Encounter

On the Tour de France, camera-toting fans are rarely in danger. The riders they're pursuing for photographs, however . . .

Giuseppe Guerini accelerates on Alpe d'Huez on July 14, 1999. Lance Armstrong *(yellow jersey)* and Richard Virenque *(polka-dot jersey)* renounce their pursuit.

For its 1999 edition, the Tour de France climbed the mythic slopes of Alpe d'Huez on July 14, the French national holiday. Every French climbing ace coveted the stage. But so did Giuseppe Guerini. The Italian launched a solo attack that left the rest of the race standing still. Nothing, it seemed, could get in Guerini's way.

The long-distance breakaway attempt of Thierry Bourguignon and Stéphane Heulot was over. The two Frenchmen were overhauled by a group of 10 riders on the opening grades of the final climb of the day: the legendary Alpe d'Huez. On this day of the 1999 Tour de France, the mountain's winner would come from this elite front group.

Guerini was promptly dropped in the opening switchbacks of the climb. The Italian, however, didn't panic. He gathered his strength, bridged back up to the leaders, and then 2 miles from the summit attacked solo off the front.

The Italian climber had been signed by the Deutsche Telekom team to assist the yellow-jersey ambitions of 1997 race winner Jan Ullrich. But the German had abandoned the Tour, leaving Guerini free to ride his own race.

Now, flying solo in the finale up Alpe d'Huez, Guerini was en route to his greatest career victory—that is, until a camera-toting fan stepped out into the middle of the road. The spectator composed his picture of Guerini, snapped his shot, and tried to move back to the sidelines, but it was too late. With the road clogged by fans and reduced to a minuscule passage, Guerini crashed straight into the hapless photographer.

"My biggest dream was turning into my biggest nightmare," Guerini said later.

The guilty spectator tried to make amends by helping the Italian back to his feet and pushing him back on course. Guerini still had a slim lead, and thankfully the rest of the climb was protected by barriers that kept the fans at bay. The Italian sprinted to the finish, notching the greatest win of his career.

And the photo? "Frankly, I don't want to see it," said Guerini.

Deutsche Telekom rider Guerini celebrates his stage win at the summit of Alpe d'Huez.

BIC
BIC
98

The Tour's Backstage

There's the Tour de France, and then there's everything that happens before, after, and around the Tour de France. From the journalists to the publicity caravan to the fans and the families of the riders, the Tour's backstage is fascinating . . .

On July 25, 1931, between Charleville and Malo-les-Bains, race leader Antonin Magne *(right)* squelches the breakaway attempt of Jef Demuysere *(left)* and Gaston Rebry.

Spy Games

A little strategy, a little spying. At the Tour de France, you do what you must to stay in the race...

To win the Tour de France, a rider must monitor his fitness, diet, and recuperation to perfection. But he must also monitor the tactics of the other race favorites. Spying is not necessary; however, if a helpful informant comes your way, well, then so be it.

At the exit of the Pyrenees, Antonin Magne wore the yellow leader's jersey of the 1931 Tour de France. But the French champion wanted just one more thing: rest. Belgian threat Jef Demuysere was inching ever closer to the race lead, and even though there were only two more days left in the Tour, an exhausted Magne knew that he would have to be vigilant to the very end.

Stretched on his hotel bed after the stage to Charleville, Magne glanced distractedly at the pile of mail spilling off his bedside table. The Frenchman's routine was to never open his mail during a race. On this occasion, however, an envelope piqued his curiosity. Bigger than the others, it was also postmarked in Belgium—the home country of his rival Demuysere.

The anonymously written letter related a conversation overheard in a Belgian café run by the parents of Gaston Rebry, one of Demuysere's teammates. Rebry's parents recounted the details of an attack their son and Demuysere were planning to launch on the stage between Charleville, Belgium, and Malo-les-Bains on July 25. That stage was the very next day, and Magne immediately understood the brewing race tactics. It was perfectly plausible that the Belgians would attempt one last Tour de France coup on the cobblestones of northern France, a terrain identical to that of their native country.

The next day, a vigilant Magne glued himself to the wheels of Rebry and Demuysere. As the letter had warned, the duo attacked. But Magne was ready to react. Despite crashing on a railroad crossing, the Frenchman refused to be dropped. Rebry may have won the stage, but Magne saved his lead in the overall race—thanks to an anonymous letter writer and talkative parents.

It was in the Pyrenees that Magne consolidated his victory at the 1931 Tour. On July 8 between Pau and Luchon, he won the stage and the race's yellow jersey.

8

Forza Italia!

Gino Bartali was a true *campionissimo* by the grace of his talent and for the honor of Italy.

Gino "the Pious" Bartali accepts a blessing from His Grace Monseigneur Pierre Marie Théas before the start of the Lourdes–Toulouse stage on July 8, 1948.

Sports and politics have sometimes made for strange bedfellows. Case in point: the 1936 Berlin Olympics, tainted by Adolf Hitler's attempts to promote Nazi ideology. Fortunately, the glory of the 1948 Tour de France and the patriotic exploits of Italian Gino Bartali exemplified how inspiring mixing politics and sports could be . . .

On July 19, 1948, after the 12th stage finish in Cannes, Gino Bartali bid his teammates good night and retired to his hotel room. At 34 years old, he needed his rest to stay competitive. Nonetheless, at the close of the 12th stage of the 1948 race, Bartali, the Tour winner in 1938, was a distant 20 minutes behind the yellow jersey, French upstart Louison Bobet.

But a phone call soon roused him. On the line was his friend Alcide de Gasperi, the leader of Italy's Christian Democratic Party. Thanks to an earlier conversation with his wife at home in Florence, Bartali was aware of the crisis brewing in his country. A political extremist had shot and injured the secretary of the Italian Communist Party, Palmiro Togliatti. The country was teetering on the verge of civil war.

"Gino, we need you," de Gasperi said over the phone.

"What can I do?" Bartali asked. "I'm racing the Tour de France. I can't come back home."

"Precisely," de Gasperi said. "You can help by winning stages. That will create a diversion and possibly reduce the tensions here."

After a long silence, Bartali responded: "I can do more than that. I'll win the Tour de France!"

The next day dawned with the first of three epic stages in the Alps. Under an onslaught of hail, Bartali devoured the Allos, Vars, and Izoard climbs, stealing 18 minutes from race leader Bobet. On the second Alpine stage, Bartali stormed into the yellow jersey. And on the third, Bartali authored his third stage win in a row, escaping solo to win in Lausanne, Switzerland.

Ten years after his first Tour de France win, Bartali won again—for Italy.

Ten years after his 1938 Tour de France triumph, Bartali won again, stealing seven stages, including the one between Lourdes and Toulouse.

Bartali wins a sprint finish in Liège on July 23.

8

Tino Makes Them Swoon

When Tino Rossi makes a Tour de France appearance, the fans—already fanatical—go giddy.

A disproportionate number of women crowded the Tour de France sidelines in Bordeaux on July 15, 1952. The female presence was not for Italian champion Fausto Coppi, who would win the race by the gargantuan margin of 28 minutes over his runner-up, Belgian Stan Ockers.

Nor were the ladies out in force for up-and-coming singer Annie Cordy. Sponsored by a brand of aperitif alcohols, Cordy would sing snippets outside bistros on the Tour de France race route. Often her concert would be broken by the honking of police cars signaling the arrival of the race. It was time for Cordy to pack up with the caravan and hustle off to the next town down the road.

On July 15, women swarmed the Tour de France for Tino . . . Tino Rossi, of course, who would be giving a free concert at the stage's finish. In 1952, the crooner cajoled the same kind of mostly female hysteria that would later be caused by the Beatles and the Stones.

To keep the crowds under control, Rossi did not travel with the publicity caravan à la Cordy. That night, he arrived by car in Bordeaux with a police escort. An estimated 80,000 fans showed up for the concert. Organizers expected the worst, but the show went off without a hitch–until the crowd dispersed.

Suddenly, a police officer spied an abandoned cradle. Inside was an infant, sleeping soundly. A young mother, so entranced by the sight of Rossi, had forgotten the very existence of her progeny.

June 30, 1952: Tino Rossi *(right)* congratulates stage winner and new yellow jersey Fiorenzo Magni in Metz.

In the first years after switching to a national-team format, the Tour de France introduced the publicity caravan to appease the private sponsors who no longer had their names branded on the team jerseys. The caravan was an immediate hit, thanks in part to occasional cameos by stars of music and cinema.

The great Fausto Coppi won the 1952 Tour de France with a 28-minute lead on runner-up Stan Ockers, of Belgium.

8

Plan of Attack

Prepare an attack down to the smallest detail. Keep the secret carefully guarded, and then have it all blow up in your face. Drat!

Louison Bobet listening to the advice of his team director, Marcel Bidot *(right)*

The Tour de France is like a game of poker: Strategy counts. And as Kenny Rogers sings, "You got to know when to hold 'em, know when to fold 'em." If you show your Tour de France cards too soon, your whole race can go up in smoke.

At dawn on July 22, 1953, French national team director Marcel Bidot opened the window of his hotel room to a surprising sight: the entire rival North-East-Central team sneaking out on a training run. Bidot was aware of the yellow-jersey ambitions of the North-East-Central team's leader, Gilbert Bauvin. Smelling that something was up, Bidot woke up his team. "An attack of some kind is being prepared," he warned. "Be on guard and don't let anyone escape."

On the day's stage, just outside of Gap, two North-East-Central riders busted off the front. Ready to react, the French team, which included overall contender Louison Bobet, sent Adolphe Deledda to join the break. The three men relayed to an advance of 10 minutes before beginning the Vars climb, the first ascension of the day.

Back in the bunch, Bobet decided to one-up his rival Bauvin. After all, thanks to the early attack by the North-East-Central formation, Bobet, too, had a support rider off the front. Bobet attacked with Jesus Lorono on the Vars climb. He then dropped the Spanish climber on the descent and soloed forth to join the trio off the front.

In the break, the North-East-Central duo decided to cut their effort and wait for team leader Bauvin. Deledda, however, informed that Bobet was about to bridge up to the front, continued his charge. The two teammates reunited at the best of all possible moments, in the flats of the Guil Valley, where Deledda set a torrid pace to tow Bobet to the foot of the Izoard climb. Nearing the base of the mountain, Deledda was running dangerously close to empty. "One more relay, Adolphe. Just one more!" Bobet pleaded. Deledda somehow found the strength. He launched a fresh Bobet onto the climb and toward his first of three consecutive Tour de France wins.

Bidot *(third from right)* with the 1953 French Tour de France team

8

De Gaulle Makes His Rounds

He's a great man, a head of state. But he's also a cycling fan, and he's come to see the Tour de France.

On July 16, 1960, in Colombey-les-deux-Eglises, the pack stops to greet Charles de Gaulle, who is shaking hands here with race leader Gastone Nencini.

On this 16th stage of the 1960 Tour de France, the race was essentially a wrap. With just two stages to go, Gastone Nencini enjoyed an insurmountable lead in the general classification ahead of his fellow Italian Graziano Battistini. The mood in the race, therefore, was relaxed. At the midpoint of the stage between Besançon and Troyes, the powerhouse teams controlled the front of the race. No riders had been allowed to launch even the smallest of escapes.

On July 16, 1960, a rumor ran rampant in the peloton: French president and World War II icon Charles de Gaulle would be at the roadside to personally give his benediction to the race. The excitement in the pack was palpable, and the good news was spread from rider to rider. Unfortunately, the message never got to French rider Pierre Beuffeuil.

It was at the exit of the town of Chaumont that race director Jacques Goddet shared the good news: Charles de Gaulle would be present at the roadside when the race reached Troyes, the town of Colombey-les-deux-Eglises, where the French president was vacationing in his country home.

Race director Goddet pulled his car to the front lines of the pack and enlisted a helping hand from reigning world champion André Darrigade and French national champion Henry Anglade. The two cyclists would ride at the front of the race with Tour leader Nencini. Their mission: to halt the race in a salute to General de Gaulle.

De Gaulle, for his part, was embarrassed. "The Tour is stopping for me?" he asked. With the peloton immobilized, handshakes were exchanged, and pictures were flashed of the French president with the leaders of the Tour de France.

Pierre Beuffeuil, a rider with the little-known Centre-Midi team, solos to victory in Troyes.

Meanwhile, at the back of the race, Pierre Beuffeuil was huffing and puffing to catch up to the pack. The Frenchman, the member of a modest regional squad, had been the victim of a mechanical mishap. Chasing alone, he had no knowledge of the meet and greet with de Gaulle. Seeing the peloton at a standstill, Beuffeuil shrugged and seized his chance. The Frenchman sprinted past the pack and charged solo to the stage win.

Henry Anglade, who would finish eighth overall, sits at the front and alongside the yellow jersey, Nencini.

July 5, 1961: Guido Carlesi wins a sprint finish ahead of Jacques Anquetil in the stage between Turin and Antibes.

The Power of the Press

**Resignation has set in.
The champion no longer believes.
But then there's a chance meeting with a journalist, and everything changes.**

Theoretically, the role of the press is to write about Tour de France tactics, not to influence the outcome of the race. Some journalists, however, let their passions get the better of them.

On the last day of the 1961 Tour de France, Italian Guido Carlesi rode like the wind, fixated on the final finish line of the race. Head down and with all his might, Carlesi distanced the pack in the finale, raging first to the finish at Paris's Parc des Princes velodrome.

The Italian's goal was not to steal the yellow jersey from Jacques Anquetil. The Frenchman had dominated the race from start to finish and was untouchable at the top of the standings. The fight for third, however, was still being waged, with Carlesi trailing Charly Gaul by just 8 seconds. Gaul was a mountain specialist. On these final flats in Paris, the rider from Luxembourg was vulnerable to Carlesi's sprinting prowess.

The night before, though, Carlesi had seemed satisfied with third. "This close to the finish, a deficit of 8 seconds or 8 minutes is really the same thing. It's impossible to make up the difference," the Italian told a journalist during an interview in his hotel room.

Another member of the press, Frenchman Roger Bastide, overheard Carlesi's comments and took him to task. Wouldn't his teammates, and Italy as a whole, be disappointed with Carlesi's lack of fighting spirit? After a short silence, Carlesi asked to redo the interview. This time, the same questions elicited completely different answers.

And the next day, sprinting away in the Parc des Princes, Carlesi secured second place in the Tour de France—2 seconds faster than Charly Gaul.

The 1961 Tour de France podium: Anquetil wins his second Tour ahead of Carlesi, who stole second from Charly Gaul on the race's final stage.

Journalist Roger Bastide *(left)* with Raymond Poulidor

8

Purple Prose

He's a gentleman, but he's also Antoine Blondin, always good for a farce and a laugh.

The legend of the Tour de France may be dictated by its riders, but it's the journalists who record the race's greatest moments for posterity. Between 1954 and 1982, Antoine Blondin, who published his prose in the pages of the French sports daily* L'Equipe*, was the most eloquent of them all.

On a dark and dreadful morning in Bordeaux in 1962, Antoine Blondin was a hungover shadow of his former self. Through the haze in his mind, the French journalist still heard the curt words of Tour de France race director Jacques Goddet, the founder of *L'Equipe* newspaper and therefore Blondin's boss.

The night before, however, the two men had returned to their Bordeaux hotel as the best of friends. Blondin's mistake was not hitting the sack straight away after an evening already high on alcohol content. At the hotel bar, several journalists were celebrating the birthday of André Gaillard, one of the daredevil motorcycle pilots whose job was to tow the journalists to the heart of the peloton.

A tipsy Blondin joined the festivities, grabbing what he thought was a drink but turned out to be an inkwell. A tiny sip was all it took to launch Blondin into a vomiting fit, and the Frenchman sullied the hotel's rich carpet and the sheets back in his room.

The hotel management complained, and Goddet, concerned for the reputation of his paper, wanted an explanation. "My dear Antoine," he said, "if I understand right, you had a bit too much ink running through your veins last night."

Blondin, cheeky in his guilt, replied, "What do you expect, Mr. Goddet? It was so that I could piss out my next article!"

Jacques Goddet *(at the wheel)*, director of both the French sports daily *L'Equipe* and the Tour de France

Writer Antoine Blondin *(far left)* embarks on the 1962 Tour de France.

8

Chalk One Up for Merckx

A night of drinking, the start of a stage, and a novice holding a chalkboard—it's a recipe for disaster.

Dominique Grimault, a novice time-split keeper, in front of Luis Ocana on the stage between Grenoble and Orcières-Merlette on July 8, 1971

The road to Tour de France victory is loaded with land mines: rival teams, leg-breaking mountains, and the wicked whim of the elements. Oh, and don't forget flying chalkboards.

"Grimault! Grimault! Do your job!" The voice shouted over the 1971 Tour de France's race radio awakened Dominique Grimault from his stupor. An apprentice journalist, the young Frenchman had been given the task of filling in as a time-split man, the chalkboard-toting official on the back of a motorcycle who flashes race stats—stage miles remaining, time splits between breaks—to the peloton.

The cub reporter was feeling sluggish after a bout of hazing from the more experienced journalists on the race. The night before, at a hotel bar in Orcières-Merlette, a group of journalists had been discussing Luis Ocana's majestic breakaway. As the rounds of drinks multiplied fast, Grimault announced that he was retiring for the night. "I'm not thirsty," he said.

"Now, why should one drink only when one is thirsty?" French press veteran Antoine Blondin asked.

Grimault shrugged and agreed to continue the party. The next morning, he was paying for it dearly. Groggy and in a hungover haze, Grimault sat slumped on the back of a motorcycle, scratching out the time splits for a breakaway launched by Eddy Merckx and his Molteni teammates. Suddenly, a gust of wind got the better of Grimault. The Frenchman lost his grip on the chalkboard, which flew in the direction of Merckx's head.

"Good God, if it hits Eddy, my career will be over before it even begins," Grimault remembered thinking.

As Guillaume Driessens, the team director of Merckx's Molteni squad, stared at Grimault with near hate, the flying chalkboard whipped toward the racers, who thanks to quick bike-handling skills, just missed getting whacked in the face.

Grimault breathed a sigh of relief. And after the French journalist endured a short barrage of Flemish expletives, the race rolled on as if nothing had happened.

Grimault was an intern journalist on the Tour de France in 1971.

8

First Lady

She's beautiful and stubborn. And her husband is a champion. Josiane Ocana gets what she wants.

Luis Ocana in 1973, alongside his wife, Josiane, who was willing to do anything to follow her husband on the Tour de France

During the month of July, the wives of Tour de France stars are resigned to three weeks of solitude, broken only by a short phone call at the end of each stage. It's the way of the race, an inevitability accepted by most of the Tour riders' spouses. But not Josiane Ocana. In 1973, Luis Ocana's wife had other ideas.

Josiane Ocana chased every stage of the 1973 Tour de France, following along in her car and listening to the exploits of her husband on the radio. The Spanish champion's luck ran dry on the first day of the race: Luis Ocana crashed when a stray dog crossed the road. But on the following stages, the Spaniard attacked. He knew that 1973 was his now-or-never chance to win the Tour de France.

Josiane wanted to share the daily emotions with her husband, but family members weren't allowed access to the Tour de France's backstage. The resourceful racing wife had an idea. While following the Tour in her car, she had taken a keen interest in the official race-route signs tacked to trees and emblazoned with an arrow and the logo of the Tour de France. After a few cuts with a pair of scissors, Josiane fashioned a makeshift VIP badge that looked remarkably like the real Tour de France thing.

With her homemade all-access credentials, Josiane was present for her husband's exploits on the July 9 stage between Méribel and Les Orres. On that day, Ocana demolished the rest of the race. Jose Manuel Fuente admitted that his overall race ambitions were over; French favorite Bernard Thévenet lost 7 minutes; and the pack—or what was left of it—straggled to the finish nearly half an hour behind the untouchable Ocana.

Finally, on the second-to-last stage of the race, a Tour official realized that Josiane's race credentials were nothing more than an amateur cut-and-paste job. But by then, it was too late. No official would dare expel the wife of the race's champion.

Ocana, the 1973 Tour winner, in the company of his wife *(right)* and Pierre Mazeaud *(left)*, the French sports minister

8

Iron Will

When the Tour de France route is put in peril by angry striking ironworkers, Jacques Goddet takes the gloves off.

On July 7, 1982, in Denain, striking workers from the Usinor factory block the Tour de France race route.

Through scorching heat, abysmal cold, or torrential rain, the Tour de France rides on, unstoppable for three weeks every July. In 1982, however, something did get in the race's way: anger.

The ninth stage of the 1982 Tour de France was a team time trial between Orchies and the tiny town of Fontaine-au-Pire. More importantly, the race would traverse the city of Denain, where the steel factory Usinor was embroiled in serious—and very public—financial difficulties. In solidarity with the workers, the Tour arranged for the team time trial to pass in front of the Usinor factory. The workers wanted the Tour to ride through the grounds of the factory itself, but the race's organizers decided that a railroad crossing would make the maneuver too risky.

At the start of the stage, a rumor began to circulate about the mounting fury of the steel workers. Race officials denied the rumor, but at the entry of Denain, a manifestation blocked the time-trial course. Twenty-four hours earlier, Usinor, the main employer of the city, had announced the elimination of 1,000 jobs.

For the distraught workers, the presence of the Tour de France was a godsend; the race created the perfect media soapbox from which the Usinor employees could shout their discontent.

"Every year, when the Tour de France is in the region, we ask for 1 or 2 hours of break time to watch the race go by," a Usinor worker said. "But now with 18 percent of us out of work, we've become the yellow jersey of unemployment."

Race director Jacques Goddet had no other choice but to cancel the stage.

Jacques Goddet *(left)* tries in vain to convince strikers to allow the Tour de France safe passage. He is forced to cancel the race's team time trial.

CHAPTER 9

Modern-Day Heroes

They are the brightest talents of the Tour de France's last 15 or 20 years. Modern-day heroes, they were sometimes overshadowed by Miguel Indurain and Lance Armstrong, but they all added a myriad of magic moments to the history of the Tour de France.

9

July 11, 1991: Thierry Marie embarks on a gargantuan solo break between Arras and Le Havre.

Marie the Magician

This land is his land. The fans chant his name. The Normandy region of France puts race-winning wings on the bike of Thierry Marie.

In 1991—and for the third time in his career—Frenchman Thierry Marie won the prologue of the Tour de France. But his race leadership would be fleeting. The Castorama rider wasn't a contender for the overall win. How long could Marie's yellow-jersey dream last?

"For me, the Tour de France was all about today," Thierry Marie said after winning the prologue time trial of the 1991 edition of the race. "That prologue has been his obsession for the past six months!" confirmed the French rider's wife, Isabelle.

But now the race was pointing toward the Normandy region of northern France, Marie's birthplace. Wouldn't it be nice, Marie began to think, to ride home with the yellow jersey?

On July 11, the race was scheduled to end in the Normandy city of Le Havre. At the start of the stage, however, Marie was no longer the race leader. The Frenchman's yellow-jersey ambitions may have been squelched, but Marie still had some fire left in his legs. Sixteen miles into the day's stage, the race encountered an intermediate bonus sprint. Marie ("without really knowing why," he later said) attacked off the front.

There was no reaction from the peloton, and Marie quickly accumulated a lead of 20 minutes. Although the Frenchman's advance continued to climb, Marie's move was considered suicidal. "He's got less than a 10 percent chance of making it to the finish," retired Tour de France great Bernard Hinault pronounced.

His blue eyes focused on the horizon, Marie pursued his effort. But 12 miles from the finish, the Frenchman's tank was running dangerously close to empty. Italian Gianni Bugno had launched a counterattack, and the rest of the race was now just 6 minutes adrift.

Marie dug deep one last time. And after 145 miles off the front—the second-longest solo breakaway in Tour de France history—the Frenchman won the day in Le Havre. Marie would get an even bigger prize that day, though. For his 6-hour escape, he was also rewarded with the yellow jersey, which he would keep on the ensuing stages through his native Normandy.

After a solo break of 145 miles, Marie is rewarded with the yellow jersey in Le Havre.

9

A Sprint Full of Drama and Trauma

With nothing to lose, a rider gives everything to win—his face included.

If Abdoujaparov had opened his eyes two seconds earlier, he might've seen the corner in time.

In 1991, Miguel Indurain began his reign at the Tour de France, deposing American Greg LeMond as the race's king. On July 28, 1991, at the race's finish on the Champs-Elysées, neither Indurain nor LeMond was the master of the show, however. That honor went to Lady Luck.

Besides the race winner, Miguel Indurain, who would remember the 1991 Tour de France with fondness? Not Greg LeMond, and certainly not the Dutch PDM team, whose ranks were decimated by a stomach virus. Maybe it would be Dimitri Konishev, winner of the race's final stage. But even that wasn't so sure.

For the sprinters of the Tour de France, there is no stage more prestigious than the final haul to Paris's Champs-Elysées—the world's most famous avenue, crowded with manic fans and swirling with the adrenaline of a mass-sprint finish.

In the final straightaway of the 1991 race, just three men were left battling for the stage: the Russian Konishev, the Uzbekistani green-jersey wearer, Djamolidine Abdoujaparov, and Germany's Olaf Ludwig. The two riders were shoulder to shoulder, but it was Abdoujaparov who was slowly pulling away—until the Uzbekistani sprinter, head down, hugged a right-hand line and rode into the metal foot of a course barrier.

Abdoujaparov flew like Superman before crashing to the ground and suffering a broken collarbone and a cranial contusion. For 14 minutes, the Uzbekistani lay on the tarmac before staggering to his feet and crossing the finish in a bid to save his green best-sprinter's jersey.

It was a heroic gesture, but it was also unnecessary. Unbeknownst to Abdoujaparov, race regulations assigned the same finishing time to all riders who crashed in the final kilometer of a stage—even in the instance of hospitalization.

Abdoujaparov crossed many finish lines first, but he never reached this one in Paris.

9

Chiappucci: Rising Star

A stage finish in Sestrières. Claudio Chiappucci had always dreamed of a Tour de France win in his Italian backyard.

Drunk with joy and drained by fatigue, Chiappucci celebrates his solo stage win in Sestrières.

The 13th stage of the 1992 Tour de France was do-or-die for Chiappucci. After being distanced in the overall standings by a failed time trial earlier in the race, the Italian was awaiting the mountains to challenge defending race champion Miguel Indurain, of Spain. On July 18, the race offered Chiappucci his dream stage: a five-mountain haul that included a summit finish at Sestrières in his native Italy.

With a marathon 145 miles still remaining in the stage, Chiappucci attacked on the very first climb. Caught once, the Italian jumped off the front again, this time with French mountain man Richard Virenque. Working a wicked climbing rhythm, Chiappucci dropped Virenque before the summit of the Iseran and powered off on a solo effort.

Far off the pace, three-time Tour winner Greg LeMond struggled at the back of the race. His face haggard and his legs leaden, the American understood that he would never win another Tour de France. LeMond would lose nearly 50 minutes before reaching the finish in Sestrières, an Italian ski station packed with close to 1 million fans—all of whom had come to see Chiappucci.

On the final climb to the finish—and after almost 7 hours solo—Chiappucci was still dancing off the front. Just two serious chasers were still in contention: defending champion Indurain and Italian Gianni Bugno. In the final miles, Bugno cracked, leaving just Indurain to continue the hunt. But the Spanish giant, fatigued and admiring the effort of Chiappucci, conceded that the day was done.

The year 1992 marked the Treaty of Maastricht and the birth of the European Union. The Tour de France celebrated the historic landmark by dipping into six neighboring nations. In Spain and Luxembourg, Miguel Indurain dominated in the races against the clock. But the Tour was now racing toward Italy and the mountains—the two loves of Claudio Chiappucci.

Drunk with exhaustion and exhilaration, Chiappucci won the stage amid his manic fans, celebrating one of the most audacious and spectacular escapes in Tour de France history.

"You drove us all to insanity!" was the headline on the next day's front page of the Italian sports daily *La Gazzetta dello Sport.*

Beaten by Chiappucci at the summit of Sestrières on July 18, 1992, Miguel Indurain nonetheless usurped the yellow jersey of the race's overall leader.

9

Emerging first from the fog, Luc Leblanc beats Miguel Indurain by a matter of meters at Lourdes-Hautacam on July 13, 1994.

Leblanc: Miracle Man

The consensus was clear: It would take a miracle to beat Miguel Indurain on the mountain stage to Lourdes.

The first Pyrenean stage of the 1994 Tour de France had just one mountain on its menu. But what a mountain it was: Lourdes-Hautacam, a lung-busting procession of steep switchbacks to the finish.

After 155 miles of warm-up flats, the first mountain stage of the 1994 Tour de France ended with an oxygen-debt spike to the finish at Hautacam. It was a decisive day for determining the overall race winner, and the peloton was giddy with anticipation. A morning breakaway attempt was reeled in on the opening grades of the climb, signaling the beginning of the real stage tactics.

Claudio Chiappucci, sick and struggling, cracked off the back. But Marco Pantani, a fellow Italian climbing ace, bulleted off the front, drawing a reaction from none other than Miguel Indurain, the race's three-time defending champion.

The Spaniard, already in yellow in this 1994 edition of the race, set a vicious cadence that, one by one, shed all of his principal rivals but Luc Leblanc. After months of nagging injury problems, the Frenchman was again in top form. Suddenly, Leblanc, who seconds ago had been on Indurain's wheel, was nowhere to be seen. Had the Frenchman suffered a flat? Had he crashed? False alarm: A thick fog had blanketed the mountain's summit, reducing visibility to just a few feet.

In an atmosphere turned majestic by the silver-tinged fog, Pantani was caught and dropped by the duo of Indurain and Leblanc. With the finish line imminent, Leblanc took his shot. Indurain latched back on after the Frenchman's first acceleration. But with the second, Leblanc edged to a narrow—and winning—gap. The Frenchman was ecstatic and exhausted at the finish. His first words: "To finish with King Miguel . . . it's incredible . . ."

Leblanc's victory at Lourdes-Hautacam was one of the greatest wins of the Frenchman's career.

9

Riis: Right on Time

Wicked weather and then a crazy race pace. It took a true Viking to rule this day.

Danish rider Bjarne Riis, victorious in Sestrières on July 8, 1996

In 1996, five-time Tour de France winner Miguel Indurain cracked out of contention in the Alps. The door to the overall victory swung wide open, and the race eagerly looked ahead to the stage between Val d'Isère and Sestrières. It was the most important day of the race. But suddenly, the stage was at risk of not happening at all.

At five o'clock in the morning on July 8, 1996, Tour de France race director Jean-Marie Leblanc opened his hotel window in the Alpine village of Tignes and saw a winter wonderland of snow–in the middle of summer!

Race organizers called an emergency meeting. On the agenda was the possibility of cancelling the stage. In 1982, a stage had been called off midrace because of strikers blocking the road (see page 201), but never in the Tour's nearly century-long history had a stage been cancelled before it even began. The first decision was to neutralize the day's opening climb, the Iseran, which was buried in snow. Next, the Galibier, its summit off-limits due to an ice storm and vicious wind, was struck from the race route. The first two mountains of the day were climbed by car.

Finally, the race start was held at Monêtier-les-Bains, just 29 miles from the stage finish in Sestrières. The peloton, fresh and revved up to ride, charged onto the Montgenèvre climb. Danish national champion Bjarne Riis, who was second in the overall standings but hungry for the yellow jersey, launched into a solo effort.

Behind the red-and-white jersey of Riis, the rest of the race tried to organize. But neither Indurain, Swiss rider Tony Rominger, nor current race leader Evgueni Berzin could bridge back up to Riis. After what amounted to a 29-mile individual time trial, Riis won at the summit of Sestrières in a time of 1 hour and 10 minutes. The Danish team Telekom rider had stolen the yellow jersey, and he would keep it all the way to Paris.

At the end of a stage cut short by bad weather, Riis usurped the yellow jersey in Sestrières. He would keep it all the way to the race's end in Paris.

9

Ullrich's Reign

So talented, yet so young, Jan looked to be cycling's next superhero.

The three jersey leaders of the 1997 Tour before the start of the July 16 Andorra–Perpignan stage: Richard Virenque *(polka-dot jersey)*, Jan Ullrich *(yellow jersey)*, and Erik Zabel *(green jersey)*.

With Miguel Indurain retired and Bjarne Riis off his mark, 1997 would perhaps be the Tour de France year of Jan Ullrich. The young team Telekom rider had been runner-up in the 1996 edition of the race. His ambition now was to become the first German to triumph at the Tour. The Pyrenees would decide his fate.

From the start of the 1997 Tour de France, Jan Ullrich quickly emerged from the shadow of his team leader, Bjarne Riis, the defending race champion. Just 23 years old, the German was a pure cycling talent. But on the morning of July 5—an epic Pyrenean stage between Luchon and Andorra—Ullrich's team director, Walter Godefroot, saw that his prodigy was almost sick with nervousness. It was an unexpected reaction from a rider renowned for his ability to keep his cool. Ullrich, it seemed, had had a realization: He could win this Tour de France.

The stage to Andorra reached its climax on the climb to the finish. The leaders had neutralized all breaks until the opening grades of the climb, where the yellow jersey, Frenchman Cédric Vasseur, jumped off the front. Suddenly, Vasseur knew his day was done. When he turned around, the Frenchman saw a terrifying sight: Jan Ullrich on his wheel, ready to attack.

Despite the difficulty of the climb, Ullrich remained seated, pushing a monster gear with Herculean strength. In contrast, Richard Virenque was dancing frantically out of the saddle, trying to match climbing wits with Ullrich. Virenque responded to the German's first acceleration but was dropped after Ullrich's second surge.

"I looked back, and there was no one left behind me," Ullrich said later. "So I kept going."

Alone at the summit finish in Andorra, Ullrich won the stage—and the race's yellow jersey.

"When I was younger, I wanted to be like [Greg] LeMond and [Laurent] Fignon. I wanted to fight for the yellow jersey," Ullrich said. "My dream has come true."

Yellow jersey Jan Ullrich climbs Alpe d'Huez on July 19, 1997.

Andrea Tafi, Jacky Durand, Eddy Mazzoleni, and Fabio Sacchi *(left to right)*. On July 19, 1998, in Montauban, Durand emerged first to win the sprint finish.

Durand: The Consummate Attacker

When it came to attacking, no one was as daring—or stubborn—as Jacky Durand. But would his persistence pay off?

Jacky Durand wasn't a sprinter. The Frenchman wasn't much of a climber either. But Durand was an attacker—one of the best the Tour de France has ever seen.

On July 19, 1998, Jacky Durand, like the rest of the pack, was thirsty. A brutal heat wave was baking the Tour de France. "It was awful. After just 25 miles, we didn't have anything left to drink," Durand said. "I dropped back to get more bottles for me and my teammates. That was the hardest part of the day, because I then had to fight my way back to the front of the pack."

The race approached the intermediate bonus sprint in Salviac, and Durand considered an attack. The Frenchman's favorite tactic was to tag along with the accelerating sprinters and then to solo off the front once the bonus-sprint line was passed. That's precisely what the two-time French national champion did, followed by five other riders. The rest of the race, still reeling from the oppressive heat, let the escape go. Occasionally, a rider or two would try their luck at joining the breakaway. All failed until Italian national champion Andrea Tafi sped away from the bunch on the short roller-coaster climbs outside Quercy. After an exhausting effort, Tafi bridged up to the break.

In Durand's mind, the dangerous Tafi was now the man to beat. "I wanted to attack alone in the final 3 miles, but it was impossible, first because of the headwind and then because of Tafi," Durand said later. "He was too strong. I think he thought he was unbeatable."

The Italian's confidence, however, got the better of him. Tafi launched the sprint a long 330 yards before the finish. It was a premature move. Sprinting with all his might, Durand nicked the Italian at the line to steal the stage.

On July 12, 1994, Durand, the reigning French national champion, won his first Tour de France stage at the end of a heroic solo breakaway.

9

Accompanied by Colombian Santiago Botero *(right)*, Erik Dekker rolls to a stage victory in Revel on July 11, 2000.

Dekker's Hat Trick

It's what they teach them in that flat country up north: Ride as fast as you can.

Four days from the finish of the 2000 Tour de France, Erik Dekker had already enjoyed a successful race. The Dutchman had pocketed two stage wins, his first-ever triumphs at the world's greatest race. In Lausanne, Switzerland, Dekker tried to make it three.

The Tour de France rule of thumb usually goes like this: The race's speed demons dominate the flat stages, which generally culminate in the chaos of a mass sprint. The mountain stages are reserved for the climbers and overall race favorites. Erik Dekker was neither sprinter nor climber. But at the 2000 Tour, the Dutchman was a winning machine. On July 8 in Villeneuve-sur-Lot, Dekker soloed to victory. Then, three days later, he won again, besting in a sprint his breakaway companion, Colombian rider Santiago Botero.

On July 19, the Tour raced from Evian, France, to Lausanne, Switzerland. The peloton, which had grown accustomed to Dekker's attacking ways, braced for another break from the Dutchman. But Dekker didn't budge. And as the race rolled into Lausanne, the peloton was still together, captained by the riders of team Telekom for their designated sprinter, Erik Zabel.

With the finish nearly in sight, Dekker finally made his move, exploding off the front in the company of Belgian Mario Aerts. The duo's advance, however, was slim, and a pack full of sprinters was breathing down their necks. The sprint in the bunch was at full force, and Dekker and Aerts were dangling just barely in the lead. Zabel began to gain ground. Wearing the green jersey of the race's best sprinter, the German overhauled Aerts, but he couldn't catch Dekker. By the skin of his teeth, the Dutchman won his third stage of the race.

July 19, 2000: Dekker, escaping just meters before the finish, skunks the peloton for a stage win in Lausanne.

9

Six years after his 1995 win in Mende, Laurent Jalabert notches another July 14 stage win, this time in Colmar.

Jaja!

For all the French riders in the pack, the July 14 stage is the one to win: There's just one national holiday. But there's also just one Laurent Jalabert.

On July 14, 2001, the Tour de France served up a roller-coaster race. Five medium-mountain hauls punctuated the route to Colmar. It was a difficult day, but one that perfectly suited several Frenchmen in the race, all of whom were eager for victory on their country's national holiday.

From start to finish, the stage was a French festival: Laurent Brochard won the first intermediate bonus sprint. His teammate Patrice Halgand padded his lead in the King of the Mountains standings by matching the leaders on the day's first climbs. Then, Laurent Roux animated the stage by jumping away on a solo attack. Four other riders joined the break, among them another Laurent: Laurent Jalabert, the leader of the CSC team and already a stage winner three days earlier in Verdun.

Some 12 miles before the finish, the five-man escape rolled onto the short but taxing grades of the Collet du Linge climb. Jalabert didn't hesitate. The Frenchman busted a move that left the rest of the riders standing still. At the finish, "Jaja" became only the fourth Frenchman in Tour de France history—after Charles Pélissier, Jacques Anquetil, and Bernard Thévenet—to win twice on July 14.

For the French riders in the Tour de France, July 14 is a race within the race. The date is France's national holiday and therefore a beacon for all the nationalists in the pack. In 1995, Frenchman Laurent Jalabert did his country proud by winning the Tour's July 14 stage. Six years later, he was still feeling patriotic.

Jalabert, winner of the polka-dot climber's jersey, was the most popular French rider in the 2001 Tour de France.

9

Zabel: The Green Giant

He's the best sprinter, unbeatable in the finale of a mass-sprint fisticuff. But one can still dream of beating Erik Zabel.

Czech rider Jan Svorada wins the final stage of the 2001 Tour. Behind him, Erik Zabel finishes second, stealing the green jersey from Australian Stuart O'Grady.

On the morning of the final stage of the 2001 Tour de France, the green jersey of the race's best sprinter was still up for grabs. The shirt rested on the shoulders of Stuart O'Grady, but the Australian's lead in the sprint competition hung by a tenuous two points.

Erik Zabel was on the cusp of Tour de France history. Winner of the race's top-sprinter prize for the previous five years, the German would stamp his name in the record books if he could win again in 2001. To reach his goal, Zabel had no choice: He would have to beat Australian speedster Stuart O'Grady on Paris's Champs-Elysées.

From the beginning of the 2001 race, Zabel had proved his sprinting prowess. The Telekom rider had won three stages, in Boulogne, Seraing, and Evry. But O'Grady had been more consistent. Because he had tallied intermediate bonus-sprint points and always competed in the mass-sprint finishes among the leaders, the Aussie had been wearing the green jersey since the eighth day of the three-week race. On July 29, the last day of the race, O'Grady owned the green jersey by two points over Zabel.

The German, however, made up the difference in the stage's two bonus sprints. Zabel moved into the "virtual green jersey," meaning it was now imperative that O'Grady beat Zabel on the Champs-Elysées to steal back the green-jersey prize.

Four hundred yards from the finish, Zabel and O'Grady duked it out on the front lines of a pack launched into the hysteria of a mass-sprint finish. Zabel or O'Grady? O'Grady or Zabel? And the stage win went to . . . Jan Svorada! The Czech sprinter surged in the finale to eke out the stage. O'Grady finished an admirable third. But tucked in for second place was Zabel. The German sealed his sixth green-jersey crown.

Svorada celebrates his stage win on Paris's Champs-Elysèes on July 29, 2001.

9 Virenque versus the Giant of Provence

Lance Armstrong seemed destined to conquer Mont Ventoux. Richard Virenque had other ideas.

Richard Virenque *(left)*, next to Cristian Moreni, leads a breakaway between Lodève and Mont Ventoux on July 21, 2002.

Back in the pack after a yearlong suspension for doping, Richard Virenque was on a quest for a sixth best-climber's prize at the Tour de France in 2002. The Frenchman launched his attack on Sunday, July 21. In front of him were the harsh, lunar grades of the Giant of Provence, Mont Ventoux. Behind him was the yellow jersey, Lance Armstrong, looking to hunt Virenque down.

Just after the start of the stage, as Richard Virenque slipped into an attack of 11 riders, the roadsides along the ascent to the Mont Ventoux summit—still 124 miles away—were already packed with fans. More than 100,000 people braved 95-degree heat to watch the race tackle the beyond-category climb to the top of the Giant of Provence.

The day's heat was comparable to the fever of frustration incubating on Virenque's Domo team. From the start of the race, Virenque had been subpar. Inconsequential in the Pyrenees, the French climber could only watch as Laurent Jalabert stole the mountain stages—and the hearts of the fans.

His ego bruised, Virenque wanted redemption on the Ventoux. Eight minutes off the front at the foot of the mythic climb, the five-time winner of the Tour's polka-dot best-climber's jersey made his move. One by one, he ditched the remaining riders in the breakaway, and 6 miles from the mountaintop finish, Virenque was all alone—alone to win or lose his stage.

Riding an adrenaline wave provided by rabid fans, Virenque dug in for what would have to be the ride of his life. Behind him, Armstrong himself was on the attack.

The American flew into a torrid chase at the base of the Ventoux, devouring the minutes that separated him from the Frenchman. But Armstrong was too far back, and Virenque was too fast. After a breakaway of 124 miles, Virenque rode to the line solo, his right index finger piercing the blue Provence sky in a victory salute.

Virenque had again earned the right to his nickname: "Richard the Lionhearted."

After resisting the return of an attacking Lance Armstrong, Virenque celebrates his victory at the summit of Mont Ventoux.

9

Fighting Frenchmen

The Tour de France is the perfect stage for a local to romance his country.

Voeckler's unlikely run in yellow transformed him from champion to hero.

In 2004, France was still awaiting a successor to Bernard Hinault, the last homegrown cyclist to win the Tour de France (in 1985). France would have to be patient: Lance Armstrong crushed his way to a sixth consecutive win, but the French did put up a good fight, notably thanks to the heroics of Thomas Voeckler and climber extraordinaire Richard Virenque.

Thomas Voeckler began the 2004 Tour in the red-blue-and-white jersey of France's national road race champion. And when the Frenchman took off that jersey, it was only to pull on the yellow of the Tour de France's overall leader—a role Voeckler would play for 10 days, despite the assaults of Armstrong and the five-time champion's U.S. Postal team.

Voeckler's wide-eyed enthusiasm made him an instant national hero. The 25-year-old knew he was no yellow-jersey match for Armstrong. But when he turned in the shirt, he exchanged it for another jersey of note: the white of the race's best young rider.

Virenque, for his part, was in a different Tour de France boat. The French veteran and six-time Tour stage winner had nothing left to prove. But he did have a record to set: an unprecedented seventh polka-dot jersey, awarded to the Tour's top climber.

At the start of the 2004 race's 10th stage, Virenque was riding on the wings of love and loss. The Frenchman's grandmother had just passed away, as had his close friend Joël Chabiron, a former team director of his Festina formation. Virenque was determined to win a stage in their memory.

From the get-go of stage 10, Virenque attacked. The motivation was there, but so were the cramps. Thirty miles into his escape, the 35-year-old was racked with fatigue. His team director urged him on, and Virenque drew inspiration from the memory of his dearly departed.

For nearly 95 miles, Virenque and fellow escapee Axel Merckx traded pulls off the front. But the son of Eddy "the Cannibal" Merckx eventually dropped off the pace, leaving just Virenque to plug away for the finish.

The Frenchman survived, crossing the line in tears of joy and fatigue. He had won a seventh climber's jersey, honored the memory of a departed friend, and dedicated a stage victory to his grandmother. And to do so, Virenque had survived a breakaway of 129 miles, 40 of which he rode all alone.

Victory for Virenque, his family, friends, country, and history.

The Armstrong Era

The Tour de France has taken on a familiar rhythm in recent years: Two hundred riders take to the start, but the same one—Lance Armstrong—wins year after year. Ever since his first triumph in 1999, the American has been virtually untouchable. Where will he stop? At five victories, like the other Tour de France greats? Or will he push the Tour de France envelope even further?

10 Remembering Fabio

One of Lance Armstrong's greatest Tour de France performances came in the guise of an homage to a fallen friend.

July 19, 1995, the day after the death of Fabio Casartelli, the pack pays its respects to the fallen champion. In the front ranks of the pack are Richard Virenque *(polka-dot jersey)*, Laurent Jalabert *(green jersey)*, Miguel Indurain *(yellow jersey)*, and Lance Armstrong *(far right)* with his teammates on the Motorola formation.

On July 18, 1995, Fabio Casartelli crashed while descending the Portet d'Aspet. Gravely injured, the 25-year-old Italian died, sending the peloton into a state of shock. Days later, Lance Armstrong paid his fallen teammate the greatest of tributes.

Lying inanimately on the roadside, Fabio Casartelli was in a deep coma after crashing on the Portet d'Aspet. The Italian Olympic road race champion at the 1992 Barcelona Games never woke up. He left behind a wife and a young child.

Frenchman Richard Virenque won that day's stage, but his triumph became an afterthought. The next day, the peloton rode the 147 miles to Pau as a funeral march. Without a single breakaway and in almost total silence, the race rolled slowly to the finish. Then, in the final straightaway, Casartelli's Motorola team came to the front of the race, crossing the finish line in symbolic unison.

The Tour de France show, however, had to go on. Two days later, Motorola rider Armstrong escaped with 11 others on the roads between Montpon-Ménestérol and Limoges. Nineteen miles from the finish, the American put on a stunning show of strength, dropping the rest of the pack in a solo bid for the stage win. "I was in a lot of pain, but the memory of Fabio helped get me to the finish," the Texan said.

No one that day could stop Armstrong. "Someone above gave him incredible strength today," Virenque said after the stage. Earlier in the race, Casartelli had singled out this stage to Limoges as the day the Italian had planned to win. As Armstrong soloed to the finish line, the American looked up, piercing the sky with two fingers. His message was clear: "For you, Fabio . . ."

Three days after the tragedy, Armstrong offers his stage win in Limoges to his fallen teammate.

10

Armstrong: Chapter One

The Tour de France was waiting for Lance Armstrong. In 1999, he scored his first yellow-jersey success.

Lance Armstrong, in front of Fernando Escartin and Ivan Gotti, climbs to Sestrières on July 13, 1999.

In the absence of its two previous winners—Jan Ullrich and Marco Pantani—the 1999 Tour de France was on the lookout for a new champion. Lance Armstrong was in the yellow jersey after the first time trial, but the American had never ranked among the race's top climbers.

After a rest day, the 1999 Tour de France hit the hills on July 13. Armstrong, the American miracle cancer survivor, was at the helm of the race. The U.S. Postal rider was back to his best. But the Texan's precancer best had never included victory at a major three-week stage race.

In 1999, however, Armstrong was a Tour de France force. The 1993 world road race champion had exploded during the 1999 Tour prologue; ditto for the individual race against the clock in Metz.

Now, with the Alps looming, Armstrong was the prime target of the race's mountain men. Kelme was the first team to launch the hostilities. On the first climb of a stage spiked with six mountain summits, the Spanish formation pushed the pace into the stratosphere.

Strong and stoic, Armstrong sat in with the climbing aces until the opening grades of the ascent to the finish at Sestrières. Ivan Gotti and Fernando Escartin, two of the most dangerous contenders for the overall race, succeeded in distancing Armstrong by a handful of seconds. Was the American in trouble or was it all a bluff?

The answer came 5 miles from the finish. In the midst of a sudden storm, Armstrong counterattacked with panache. Swiss rider Alex Zülle latched on, but Armstrong didn't even notice. In a race-winning trance, the American accelerated again, busting free to win the day. A Tour de France champion was born.

Armstrong wins his first mountain-summit stage of the Tour de France at Sestrières.

IO

Lance Armstrong *(left)* and Jan Ullrich *(center)* eye each other up on Alpe d'Huez. The Texan, paced by his teammate Jose Luis Rubiera, is on the cusp of attacking.

The Look

Just how strong was Lance Armstrong? The American looked as if he was weakening. Or was he just putting on a poker face?

On July 17, 2001, Lance Armstrong was having a very bad Tour de France day. The cancer survivor and winner of the past two Tours was in difficulty every time the road went up. After dangling at the back of the pack on the ascension of the Glandon, Armstrong was again hurting on the Madeleine, a grimace smeared across his face. Excitement began to bubble among the rest of the race favorites.

There was no more time to lose. Lance Armstrong had already ceded more than half an hour to a group of 14 riders that had escaped two days earlier on the roads to Pontarlier. But now the race was at the foot of the mythic Alpe d'Huez climb. Everyone expected Armstrong to attack. The American, however, looked out of sorts.

Jan Ullrich assembled his Telekom team at the front of the race. The German whipped his squad into action, setting a torrid pace he hoped would soon leave Armstrong floundering. But at the base of Alpe d'Huez, the American was still hanging on.

And then, just after the first of Alpe d'Huez's 21 switchback turns, Armstrong attacked. His bluff played, the American turned and stared directly into Ullrich's eyes. His message: "Catch me if you can." Ullrich could not. The German was left standing still as Armstrong charged onto the climb.

Up ahead was just Frenchman Laurent Roux, who was fading fast after a daylong breakaway attempt. "When Armstrong passed me, I had the impression he was on a motorcycle," Roux said after the finish. "That's how fast he was going."

Winner of the Alpe d'Huez stage—and eventually the whole 2001 Tour—Armstrong had literally toyed with the rest of the race. "All the team directors have a TV in their cars," he explained. "I wanted to make them think that I was having an off day to force them to set the pace. In reality, I was feeling just fine!"

Armstrong attacks, winning solo at the summit of Alpe d'Huez on July 17, 2001.

10

The Rabbit and the Panda

Laurent Jalabert dashed off on his own, thinking he could escape Lance Armstrong.

July 18, 2002: Laurent Jalabert embarks on a marathon mountain solo attack.

Lance Armstrong seemed destined to win the 2002 Tour de France before it even began. Having won the three previous editions with remarkable ease, the American was the untouchable favorite of the race. But this year, Armstrong had been beaten by Colombian Santiago Botero in the race's first time trial. Was the Texan vulnerable? On July 18, Frenchman Laurent "Jaja" Jalabert went looking for the answer.

Jaja (also nicknamed "the Panda" for his dark eyebrows and sympathetic facial features) had made an announcement midway through the 2002 Tour de France. The Frenchman would retire at the end of the season, closing his career at 34 years of age and with 138 professional wins on his race résumé.

On July 18, the riders of the Tour de France–the last in Jalabert's career–had a rude awakening as they butted up against the first mountains on the three-week race route: Jalabert escaped with a handful of riders on the grades of the Aubisque climb. At the mountain's summit, Jalabert was alone off the front. The Frenchman then gobbled the Soulor climb and, bolstered by the manic cheers of his fans, began to believe in the possibility of a Pyrenean stage win.

Eight miles from the finish and with just the Mongie climb to go, Jalabert got bad news. Back in the bunch, Armstrong was counterattacking in the company of his U.S. Postal lieutenant Roberto Heras. The race between the rabbit and the Panda was on.

Whacked by the heat and fatigued by his colossal solo effort, Jalabert looked over his shoulder. There in the distance, he saw Armstrong closing in fast. When the American caught Jalabert, the two men exchanged glances. "I saw in his eyes that Armstrong was almost feeling sorry for me," Jalabert said later. "I think he was even disappointed that I wouldn't have the chance to win the stage."

The Frenchman was out of gas. Jalabert finished ninth on the stage–a day won by Armstrong, who would try on yet another yellow jersey.

Jalabert, happy but exhausted, finishes ninth on a stage won by Lance Armstrong.

10

Show Time

Nervous riders make for scary—and theatrical—finales.

A crash during a sprint finish can ruin the race for everyone who follows.

The 2003 Tour de France was meant to be the greatest show in the race's history. It was the 100th birthday of the world's most prestigious bike race, first won in 1903 by Frenchman Maurice Garin. To celebrate its centenary, the 2003 Tour started with a bang.

On July 6, 2003, the first stage of the race traced a flat, sprinter-friendly 104 miles between Saint-Denis and Meaux. The first week of the Tour is traditionally fraught with nerves; the peloton is still fresh, and the flatland specialists of the race jostle recklessly for early glory.

In the final straightaway of the stage, the race had ratcheted up to 43 miles per hour when, suddenly, José Enrique Gutierrez, of Spain, touched wheels with another rider and plummeted to the road. Like dominoes, three-quarters of the peloton piled to the ground, including the yellow jersey, Australian Bradley McGee, winner of the previous day's prologue. Four-time race champion Lance Armstrong was also caught up in the tumble.

True, crashes are par for the course during the Tour de France's first week, but rarely had the consequences been this serious. Although the majority of the crash victims escaped with little more than swaths of road rash, Frenchman Jimmy Casper lay on the roadside with an injury to his spine. He would stay in the race but with a brace strapped to his neck.

American contender Levi Leipheimer and Dutchman Mark Lotz were forced to abandon the race. Leipheimer had suffered a hip injury; Lotz, facial lacerations.

Tyler Hamilton, another American, on the Danish CSC squad, miraculously stayed in the race. Hamilton had cracked his collarbone in the crash. Nevertheless, he gritted through the pain and finished the 2003 Tour de France a stunning fourth overall.

Casper appeared to be out with spinal injuries, but he fought to race on.

IO

All-Terrain Tour de France

The Tour leader goes off course to stay in the race.

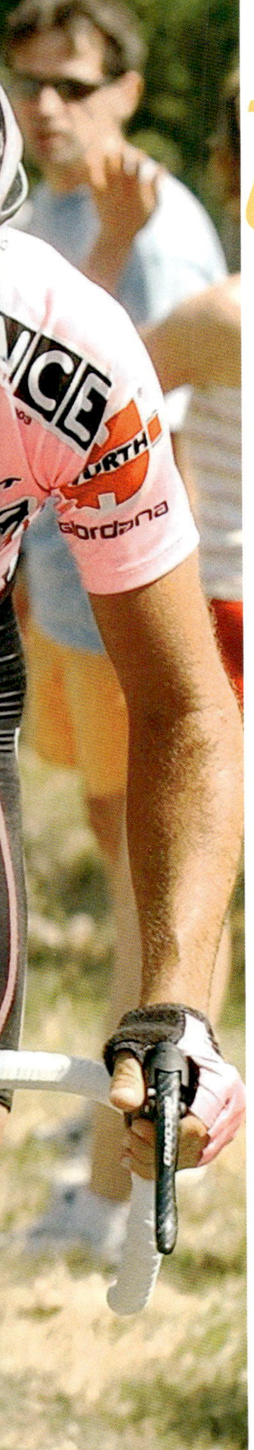

On July 14, 2003, the weather was as hard as the Tour de France race route. A stabbing sun scorched the roads and riders, writing a race script that would be one of the most spectacular—and cruel—in Tour history.

The stage started with a breakaway of 20 riders, a move quickly squelched by the U.S. Postal team, which policed the pack for its leader and then four-time Tour de France champion, Lance Armstrong. But like the rest of the pack, the American team was burned by the heat; they lost their reins on the race and allowed a new 14-man escape to bubble free.

Off the front and approaching the day's finish in Gap, the breakaway dissolved into mutiny, with each man looking out for his own interests. The pack was back in the game and being led by Armstrong, who was navigating a descent on the wheel of Spanish overall threat Joseba Beloki.

The sinewy road had been baked to a sticky mess by the summer sun; the asphalt was literally melted in sections. Beloki braked too hard through a turn. His rear wheel pitched sideways, and the Spaniard slammed sickeningly to the tarmac in a multiple-fracture crash.

Armstrong, glued to Beloki's wheel, had nowhere to go. The American swerved off the road and into a field, involuntarily forced into the sport of cyclo-cross. After riding through the field and over a ditch, Armstrong was back on track, and he rejoined the front of the race.

That ninth stage of the 2003 Tour was won by Alexandre Vinokourov, of Kazakhstan. But the fact that Armstrong finished the day in one piece and with the yellow jersey still on his shoulders . . . well, that was a miracle.

Armstrong's keen eye on Beloki allowed him to dodge trouble.

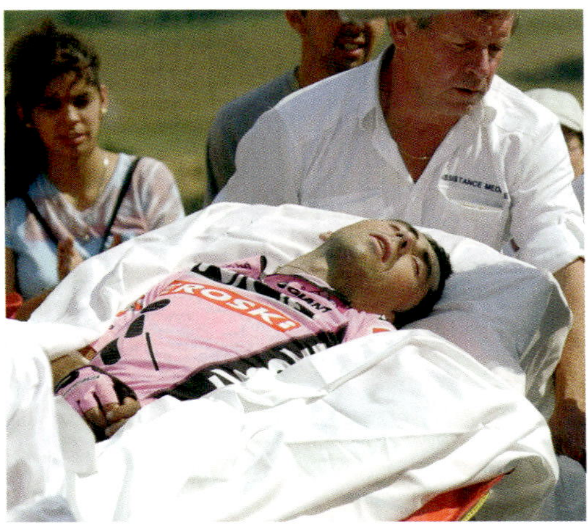

Beloki's tour was finished with a broken leg and crushed spirit.

Down to the Wire

"The race of truth" revealed who would win the Tour this year.

Ullrich starts the time trial confident...

July 26 was the decisive day of the 2003 Tour de France. It was the stage that would swing the balance between Jan Ullrich and Lance Armstrong, the latter bidding to become only the fifth rider in history to win the world's toughest bike race five times. It was the final time trial of the Tour, and on the morning of the race, Armstrong and Ullrich were separated by just 65 seconds in the overall standings.

Sixty-five seconds over 28 miles—the deficit would have been impossible for most riders to overcome. But Ullrich was a race-against-the-clock specialist. Twice he had earned the title of world time-trial champion, but the German was desperately seeking his first Tour de France win since 1997.

Ullrich raced no-holds-barred. He equipped his bike with carbon-spoked wheels, an aerodynamic choice that could turn disastrous if there was too much wind. Armstrong chose a more conservative route, adding only a simple triathlon-style handlebar to his standard time-trial machine.

On the course, Ullrich caused a sensation. Churning a monster gear (55 x 11) and dipping deep into his physical reserves, the German gave Armstrong a run for his Tour de France money.

Meanwhile, the time-trial road to Nantes in northwestern France had turned treacherous, slicked by torrential rains. Armstrong was forced to take risks to keep the German in check, but if the American were to crash, he would almost certainly tumble to second place overall.

Fate, however, dealt the tumble to Ullrich. The Team Bianchi rider lost traction in the course's 12th roundabout and with the finish line tantalizingly close. The German—shocked but relatively unscathed—rebounded quickly and continued the race. But his morale was lost—as was his shot at the yellow jersey. At the finish, Ullrich finished 11 seconds off of Armstrong's pace. The American had joined the exclusive club of five-time Tour de France winners, after Jacques Anquetil, Eddy Merckx, Bernard Hinault, and Miguel Indurain.

Ullrich, in turn, garnered comparisons to Raymond Poulidor, the Tour de France's "eternal second." Once again, Ullrich was runner-up to Armstrong.

...but his crash is the end of his hopes of winning.

Armstrong and Simeoni: A Love Story

Armstrong exerts his authority as "patron of the peloton."

With every professional cyclist comes a full package: his ego, his demons, his triumphs, his failures. Usually the emotions are kept out of the limelight, but occasionally a quarrel becomes public. Take, for example, the 2004 Tour de France and this rare and stupefying spectacle: an overall race favorite personally chasing down an unknown rider solely to prevent him from winning a stage . . .

There was no love lost between Lance Armstrong and Filippo Simeoni. The Italian had provided damning testimony at the doping trial of Michele Ferrari, a doctor with a dubious reputation who counted Armstrong among his clients. Armstrong didn't appreciate Simeoni's testimony, and their relationship has since been marked by a mutual disrespect.

So when Simeoni joined a breakaway during the 2004 race, it was Armstrong himself who launched off in pursuit of the Italian, ordering him back to the peloton. Putting his pride in his pocket, Simeoni obliged . . . temporarily.

The Italian again bubbled off the front on the Tour's last day, a stage usually ridden at a parade's pace, as the riders revel in a race survived. Again, Armstrong and the U.S. Postal team shadowed and squelched Simeoni's every move.

To this day, war is still being waged between the two cyclists. Simeoni has filed suit against Armstrong for his strong-arm Tour de France tactics, and Armstrong, in turn, has accused Simeoni of defamation.

Simeoni's breakaway attempt is covered by none other than the race leader.

Armstrong and Simeoni discuss their tumultuous history.

More than a million people lined the course of Alpe d'Huez.

The Untouchable

The crown jewel of the 2004 Tour belongs to Lance Armstrong.

On the eve of the decisive uphill time trial to the summit of Alpe d'Huez, the door to the overall crown in the 2004 Tour de France was left open, if just a crack, by Lance Armstrong. The American counted an advance of just 85 seconds over Italian Ivan Basso, the only rider remaining in the hunt for the yellow jersey.

Armstrong had his time-trialing prowess to thank for his lead in the general classification; the Texan was a locomotive in the race against the clock. But this time trial butted up against one of the most daunting climbs on the Tour de France menu. To make matters worse for Armstrong, Basso had proved to be the American's equal in the previous mountain stages of the 2004 race.

With the Tour's end just around the corner, the Alpe d'Huez climb would be the race of truth, the factor determining who would win the yellow-jersey spoils.

For weeks, fans had been making the pilgrimage to Alpe d'Huez, and on the morning of the time trial, every inch along the climb was smothered with spectators. In the finale of the climb, riders were protected by barriers on both sides of the road. But the first part of the climb was left open to the mercy of the fans, a decision that Tour de France organizers later admitted was a mistake.

In 2003, don't forget, Armstrong had crashed on Luz Ardiden in the Pyrenees after a close encounter with a fan—an accident that could have cost the American the overall race.

This time on Alpe d'Huez, Armstrong scuttled to the summit without incident. He devoured the mountain, catching and dropping Basso and winning the stage 1 minute and 1 second better than his perennial yellow-jersey rival, Jan Ullrich, of Germany.

Four stages still remained in the 2004 Tour de France, but after Alpe d'Huez, there was no question: The yellow jersey was signed, sealed, and delivered in the name of U.S. Postal leader Lance Armstrong.

Armstrong's speed up the mountain was record-breaking.

ALM. BRAND
Škoda
cervélo

History Is Made

Lance Armstrong makes a bold bid for an unprecedented seventh Tour title. With his retirement announced, it is the last chance for his adversaries to beat him. Can Armstrong withstand the onslaught, or will he finally fall?

II

Livestrong

In 2004, Armstrong won everything. Can he go even farther?

In 1996, Lance Armstrong's career—or rather his life—stopped. He was struck by cancer while on the way up: At 26, the talented classics racer was already sixth in the world rankings. He sat out the 1997 season for treatment, but just a year and a half after his diagnosis, Armstrong returned to racing, at the 1998 Ruta del Sol. He placed 15th, which would have been a miracle in itself had he stopped there. But of course he didn't stop, and nothing would stop him in the years to come.

Before the 2003 Tour, just four racers had ever won five Tours de France. In 2003, Lance Armstrong became the fifth to achieve that feat, joining Jacques Anquetil, Eddy Merckx, Bernard Hinault, and Miguel Indurain. Each cycling great had his own merit, but Armstrong outclassed the others on one front: He was the only one who had defeated a life-threatening illness before he defeated his human opponents.

The motivation behind his cycling accomplishments could not be fully understood. Perhaps it came from the stolen season of 1997, during the darkest hours of his cancer treatment. Wherever it began, it reached its pinnacle in 2004, when he went for and achieved a sixth Tour de France victory to become the race's winningest cyclist ever. But without more records to break, Armstrong's motivation suffered in 2005. Alone at the top, he had no more carrots dangling before him, only the challenge of winning a seventh Tour for himself. Would that drive, the desire to win above all else, serve him for a seventh Tour as it had served him to beat cancer?

It bears noting that none of the five-time winners retired at the top: All tried for a sixth win, and all lost. Armstrong had already beaten that curse. What did he gain by going for another Tour win? Known for starting preparations in early winter, Armstrong instead waited until midspring to announce his intentions to race again. He did not intend this bid to be just a farewell; as always, he intended to win.

Here comes the sixth victory!

Lance Armstrong becomes a legend and celebrates it on the world's most beautiful avenue.

II

Objective: Armstrong

The 2005 Tour de France—it is Armstrong's adversaries' last chance to dethrone him.

Jan Ullrich, leader of his pink army, wants to steal Armstrong's throne.

From 1999 to 2004, Lance Armstrong raced six Tours de France, and he stood on six podiums in yellow. In 2005, Armstrong was above even the grandest champions of the race's history. The smart decision would have been to retire on top. But Armstrong announced his intentions to seek an unprecedented seventh title, and he upped his own ante by declaring that, win or lose, he would retire after this Tour.

After a late start and much speculation about poor form and motivation, Lance Armstrong dove into Tour preparations with his characteristic meticulousness and zeal, attending training camps, embracing new technology, and, above all, working with that devoted Tour-winning machine of a team.

The other racers were not thrilled by the news of Armstrong's return. Their best chance to beat him had come in 2003, and still they had failed. Even after arriving late into the game and undertrained, Armstrong was immediately tabbed the favorite, except for one perennial challenger: Jan Ullrich, leader of the T-Mobile team.

Always a threat to win, Ullrich had battled his weight, motivation, team managers, and numerous other foes while trying to match his breathtaking 1997 victory. With a strong team and a renewed focus, Ullrich knew the 2005 Tour was his last chance to beat the man called "the Extraterrestrial." A win would deliver on the promise of repeating that 1997 victory and establish him as the man who dethroned the legend. Despite the presence of other talented riders, such as Ivan Basso and Iban Mayo, the members of T-Mobile were seen as Armstrong's best challengers. With three potential leaders—Ullrich, Andreas Kloden, and the always-attacking Alexandre Vinokourov—T-Mobile had the firepower to challenge Armstrong, if only the team would work together. Ullrich and others assured the media that there would be no infighting; the goal was to beat Armstrong, and the strongest rider on the team would have the support to do the job.

Armstrong with Sheryl Crow after his seventh—and final—win.

II

Armstrong Sets the Record Straight

"The Extraterrestrial" has successfully started the race...

There was no shortage of racers hoping to dethrone Lance Armstrong. For six years, they'd tried and failed. And they knew Armstrong wouldn't be back to the Tour again. Hence the tension around the Tour's first stage on July 2, 2005, a short individual time trial. The conventional wisdom was that it was too short to produce meaningful time gaps. But it was long enough to learn who would challenge to set the record straight.

Lance Armstrong was never much for conventional wisdom, and he set quickly to work dispatching his challengers—in particular, Jan Ullrich. Ullrich had said all spring that he was looking forward to a final showdown, even asserting that he would be able to beat his arch nemesis. But Armstrong gave him quick proof to the contrary: In just 12 short miles, Armstrong demolished the German, beating him by 1 minute and 8 seconds, an eternity in a race where the winning margin after 21 stages is often less than 5 minutes total. In Ullrich's defense, he had crashed into his team manager's car while training the day before and received several stitches. Seemingly, he was cursed.

None of the major challengers—Ullrich or Ivan Basso—held his own against Armstrong's remarkable onslaught. The only one who limited the damage was the Kazakhstani from the T-Mobile team, Alexandre Vinokourov. The damage was more mental than physical—a minute can, after all, be gained back quickly in the mountains—but to be punished like that from the starting ramp does not argue well.

Ullrich was perhaps the most discouraged, and understandably so. Did his training crash hurt him more than he let on? We may never know. But it seemed apparent that he would never challenge his biggest opponent. T-Mobile's hopes fell to Vinokourov. If the team would support him, perhaps they could topple Armstrong from his pedestal, or at least make him stumble. But for that, Ullrich would have to swallow his pride.

The 2005 Tour de France's first stage: In only 12 miles, Lance Armstrong stuns his competitors.

Alexandre Vinokourov, from the T-Mobile team, will finish third in this race against the clock, just 1 minute behind Armstrong.

II

On July 3, 2005, Thomas Voeckler, the French public's favorite, is quite happy with what he has done since the beginning of this Tour.

Another Jersey for Thomas Voeckler

Thomas Voeckler is well known for his jokes, but he is less known for his collections.

It was in 2004 that he had the thought to start collecting prestigious jerseys. Already in the tricolored jersey of the French national champion, he entered a fortuitous break on the Tour de France's fifth stage that landed him in the yellow race leader's jersey, which he valiantly defended for 12 days. After that, he wore the white best young rider's jersey. What would he do for an encore?

At the 2005 Tour, on just the race's second stage, Thomas Voeckler launched another opportune attack. It had little hope of succeeding, but Voeckler had another goal: to win the tiny climb of the Côte du Lac de la Vouraie, where the race's first jersey for best climber was on offer.

A long break, even if not successful in the end, would net the Frenchman the jersey as long as he was first over the climb. So break he did, for 100 miles in a group of four. Despite attacks from other riders, Voeckler cagily responded with just enough effort to stay on the wheel, then launched his own strike a mere 100 yards from the summit. The jersey was his. The break was not as successful: It was caught just 4 miles from the finish line. But Voeckler's work was done, his goal accomplished.

And even though he lost the King of the Mountains jersey the very next day, for one day it was his, another jersey in the collection.

With the retirement of Laurent Jalabert and Richard Virenque, the French needed a new cycling hero: Enter Thomas Voeckler. An opportunist par excellence, his willingness to gamble had produced remarkable feats. Voeckler claimed his legs were not strong enough to land him on the final podium in Paris in 2005, but he would do everything possible to be the race's chief agitator.

Voeckler in 2004, wearing one of the jerseys he collects: the white one, which designates the best young rider

II

Boonen's Misfortune

Boonen's second skin is green. Nothing can stop him except . . .

Among the sprinters, there was no one to monitor more closely than Belgian Tom Boonen. In April 2005, he won two classics: the Tour of Flanders, one of the sprinters' favorites, and the Paris-Roubaix race, the queen of the classics. During this last one, he dominated his rivals in a way not seen since fellow Belgian Johan Museeuw was on the scene.

Team manager Patrick Lefévère's ambition for the 2005 Tour de France supported his protégé's abilities: to land the green jersey of the race's best sprinter. The team was fully focused on this goal, and the first week of flat stages and fast finishes was essential to its realization.

But the Tour often has surprises in store. No sooner had Tom Boonen become sprinting's fastest rising star than he was sidelined by a toothache. It was so painful that it kept him awake at night, and he considered not starting the 2005 Tour. In desperation, he visited a nearby dentist to fix the problem on the race's first day.

He finished 40th in the opening time trial. There would be no yellow jersey for him, but the question really was this: Would he rebound from the episode? In a sport in which races are decided by a tire's width, would the toothache spell the difference between victory and second place? With Alessandro Petacchi and Robbie McEwen in the mix, Boonen would face the world's best sprinters, all bent on victory. The question was answered the very next day, when Boonen took a wild sprint on the second stage, and he won another the next day.

In the second stage of the 2005 Tour, Tom Boonen wins a sprint victory to clinch the green jersey. He'll win another the next day.

No one could take the green jersey from the big Belgian—no one but misfortune, that is. On July 13, he hit a wall and hurt his knee. Like most racers, he was loath to abandon the race, but pedaling caused extreme pain, and he could not start the next day. His Tour was over, and his chance to win the green jersey would have to wait another year.

Boonen is forced to abandon the race on July 13, 2005.

II

The Naked King

Armstrong is not the kind of person who would smile about a competitor's rotten luck.

On July 6, 2005, at the beginning of the fifth stage, Lance Armstrong resigned himself to wearing the jersey worn by his unlucky adversary the day before. After all, he had really played fair.

Dave Zabriskie had pulled out all the stops. First, his CSC team director, Bjarne Riis, gave him an early start time in the race's first stage, a 12-mile time trial. Riis, a cagey strategist, knew the coastal winds would pick up in the afternoon for the short time trial to Noirmoutier-en-Isle and that an early start for a time-trial specialist like Zabriskie might net a fast payoff for the team. It did, as Zabriskie flew down the course for a 2-second victory over Armstrong. He wore the yellow jersey with panache during the first stages of the Tour. His disarming charm and obvious talent as a racer energized fans, who appreciated the departure from the normal Tour script. However, for the fourth stage, Zabriskie was said to be dead meat. Armstrong and his Discovery team, dominant during the team time trials, were favored to relegate him back to the peloton's anonymity.

But CSC, galvanized by the yellow jersey, fought back. At intermediate time checks, the two teams were almost tied on time, and at the last check, CSC had 2 seconds on Discovery with only 4 miles to ride. Then, disaster struck. Just under a mile from the finish, Zabriskie crashed hard while exiting a corner. Miraculously, no one else fell, and the CSC train continued to cruise to the finish. Zabriskie, in his torn yellow jersey, was left to struggle in on his own. To add insult to injury, CSC lost the stage to Discovery. The next day, Armstrong refused to wear the yellow jersey, despite having driven Discovery to the quickest team time trial in Tour history, at an average of 35.61 miles per hour.

Just four stages into the 2005 Tour, Lance Armstrong was already in the race lead, but the customary yellow leader's jersey was nowhere to be seen. Armstrong had refused to wear it, out of respect. To Armstrong, it would have been unfair to take a jersey he did not earn, and he felt it belonged to David Zabriskie, the Tour's unlikely leader during the first week.

Tour officials pressed him, citing the rules, but Armstrong demurred. He wanted to pay homage to a long-standing Tour tradition, whereby a rider does not assume the yellow jersey when it is lost through misfortune. But Tour officials would not be swayed: Wear yellow, they said, or you're out of the race. Armstrong pulled it on. But Zabriskie, bandaged and back in CSC's red and white, still had the aura of his lost jersey.

On July 5, David Zabriskie fell and lost the yellow jersey to Armstrong. Despite being wounded, he was present at the beginning of the next stage.

II

Jan Ullrich on the finish line July 23, 2005, the Tour's second-to-last stage: He gave his all.

For a Fistful of Seconds

Jan Ullrich will not win this Tour. In all likelihood, he will not even be on the podium. His only hope is the last race against the clock.

On July 23, 2005, the Tour was nearing its end, and Lance Armstrong was practically certain to become the happiest retired person in all the United States. Barring accidents, his seventh victory was all but sewn up. But the fight for the other two spots on the podium, at the time held by Ivan Basso and the surprising Michael Rasmussen, was about to heat up.

Jan Ullrich was ranked fourth, more than 2 minutes behind Michael Rasmussen. At this next-to-last stage, an individual time trial, it was Ullrich's only chance to make a run at the podium. Two minutes and 12 seconds would be difficult to gain in just 34 miles, but Ullrich would try his hardest. Known for pushing huge gears, he would undoubtedly gain time on Rasmussen, whose strength was in the mountains. The question was whether Rasmussen could withstand the onslaught. On a hilly course, it seemed possible.

Basso's second place was likely unreachable, but Ullrich's time splits were the fastest of the day. Rasmussen, who started after Ullrich, knew the pace he would have to keep to preserve his position. But from the beginning, he failed. At the first intermediate time check, he had lost 1 minute and 58 seconds of his lead. Rasmussen knew he had lost, and he cracked, crashing twice on descents and changing his bike three times.

Ullrich continued to motor ahead, convincingly passing Rasmussen at the second time check and setting the fastest time of the day to that point. Basso's overall time may have been unreachable, but a stage victory was not. Only Armstrong, Ullrich's longtime nemesis, would undo the German's power. As had happened in so many time trials over the years, Ullrich was the best, save one. He had now finished the Tour on the podium eight times. It is a nice record, but he has only won once. Maybe he will win the Tour again now that the big boss has retired.

Michael Rasmussen breaks down during the race against the clock.

II

On July 24, 2005, Armstrong is on the podium's top step for the seventh time in a row. On his left is Ivan Basso, ranked second, and on his right is Jan Ullrich, ranked third.

The Tour, Forever

It is done! The most yellow rider in Tour history has won his seventh victory.

Lance Armstrong managed to end his career in a blaze of glory. His fans regretted his decision to retire, but they were treated to the sight of the champion standing atop the 2005 Tour podium for a record seventh time, donning yellow, and declaring, "Vive le Tour, forever."

The last stage of the Tour is always one of tradition: The racers celebrate the accomplishment of finishing the Tour by riding onto the Champs-Elysées, the most famous street in the world. The melancholy, rainy weather of the 2005 edition suited Armstrong's nostalgia. It was his last race, his zenith, a moment he had to savor more than any other. He was not concerned by the final stage; he had nothing else to prove, only a title to receive—the crowning achievement of a whole career.

But the road, wet because of the rain, was slippery, and though Armstrong was content to cruise easily to the finish, other racers were intent on securing a final win and upped the pace. Three of Armstrong's teammates fell just before crossing the Seine River, and Armstrong himself nearly met with disaster.

After the usual series of attacks and counterattacks on the treacherous cobbles of the Champs, the race was nearing its customary final sprint when Alexandre Vinokourov launched one final attack to steal the stage and even move up a place in the overall standings. Armstrong celebrated his victory with his teammates in the traditional postrace lap on the Champs-Elysées. "That is the way I wanted to end my career," he said. "It is very moving."

With his seven fingers up, one for each yellow jersey won, he could enjoy the reward for his efforts. He shared his victory with his family and teammates, who wore yellow wristbands for the occasion. On his path, there were cheers and applause, but also some shouts of, "Cheater!" Armstrong waited until he reached the podium to respond, during a historic address never before allowed to a racer.

Wearing his yellow jersey, he climbed to the top step of the podium. "Finally, the last thing I'll say for the people who don't believe in cycling—the cynics, the skeptics—I'm sorry for you," Armstrong said. "I'm sorry you can't dream big, and I'm sorry you don't believe in miracles. But this is one hell of a race; this is a great sporting event, and you should stand around and believe."

E

F

G

H

I

J

K